Where
Rivers
Converge

A publication by

Three Rivers Writers

This publication is made possible by the support of the Carver County library system, which provides a home base for the Writers' Group and the Authors' Collective, both meeting monthly at the Chanhassen, MN Library. They combined forces to create the non-profit Three Rivers Writers. Thanks also to Arts Consortium of Carver County for its continuing encouragement of all aspects of creative communication.

Send correspondence to:

Three Rivers Writers

216 Cardinal Court, Chaska, MN 55318

carvercountywriting anthology@gmail.com

Table of Contents

About this Anthology

This book is made possible by authors from the Chanhassen MN Writer's Group and The Author's Collective. Both groups meet monthly at the Chanhassen library. We hope you'll enjoy reading it as much as we enjoyed creating it.

We've become a strong writing community with a variety of goals. Right from the start we envisioned this publication as a snapshot of where we are today in our craft; a mix of artists ranging from new writers to long-time published authors.

What we share is a love of language, and a dedication to writing. We are generous in encouraging each other. Our groups are collaborative and informative. They give us a place to talk shop, share ideas, and build our knowledge of the craft.

This book is a reward for all the hours and creative energy we've spent at computer keyboards. So much good work lives only in hard drives, or filing cabinets. We thought we'd give some really good voices a chance to be heard.

We hope it inspires other writers to join us, or one of the many writing groups out there. Or start your own group. You'll be glad you did.

*A special thanks goes out to Jim Kane, Ann Jackson and Doug Munson for volunteering countless hours to create this book. We'd also like to thank the authors who so generously offered their work to make this book possible.

Excerpt from "Beatrice"

Fiction: Becky Liestman

I remember years ago, years past years. We were living here then, Alfred and me. We liked it. Our forty acres. A little bit of a farm, just as much as we could afford. We worked hard to make something of this place. We'd plant a few rows of corn and some potatoes, a real harvest we'd have. I liked lima beans best. Alfred hated them, but that didn't matter to me. He didn't have to eat them. Didn't even put them on his plate; I was that kind of wife. I'd sneak off to the kitchen, when he was out getting in the wood, or down to Fred's house for some talk, and make up my own beans, warm to the mouth and hot with summer smiles. Even then I was full of spit and vinegar, but I was smart too, just like I am now. And I'd keep it to myself. There's nothing anybody can take away from you if you keep it to yourself. I'm pleased at that.

Some days I think I'm as old as old can be. Maybe not, though. It's just that I dream right into the before's and after's, only coming up for air now and then. Most of the world's in a person's head, anyway. Always is and always has been. Why, I can sit right here and conjure up anything I want. No need to go out.

Take my husband, Alfred. He was a funny one. Tall and skinny as a fly swatter. And talk! He talked out loud, lots.

I'd rather talk to myself, like now. I figure I'm pretty good company. Not Alfred. He liked the company of others. Nothing tickled him as much as having a few of his friends over, working on a new fence or something, and talking to beat the band. You'd think his teeth would fall out, just from the shock of all that clattering and chattering, shooting out word after word. That's why I grabbed him, fresh out of lumber camp. I couldn't get over it. All that talk. How'd he come up with it? I had to marry him and find out. Never did clear up the mystery, though. After a while, I'd spend my time guessing what he'd say next, I knew him so well. Got it right most of the time, too. Didn't amount to much. Loose chatter about the new horse Doc Olson got, or there was cutworms in the tomatoes, or the new calf at the Halbertson's came hard, had to noose it around the feet and tug it out. That kind of talk.

Oh, Alfred was all right. Just wasn't deep. Could throw a penny in him and it'd hit bottom right away. I missed him a lot at first. Takes a while to get used to any kind of change. Soon though, I felt free of making so many dinners, so many lunches, so much breakfast. Full meals too. And every single one of them had to have potatoes. Alfred demanded it. It got so that I was so sick of potatoes I could hardly see straight. No time off for good behavior. A prison sentence, I always thought it was. After Alfred died, I could eat when I wanted, what I wanted. I'd often pop a few kernels of corn and that'd be it for me. Or chew on a big slice of watermelon, in season. Freedom.

I do miss his sharp angles in bed, I don't know why. Crisscrossing the thing like an x. And his just being there, talking about next to nothing by the fire in the evening. He was a good man, Alfred was. A good companion. Filled space real nice, Alfred did. Made a house a home.

Now when I lack companionship I just imagine him right back in his rocking chair by the kitchen fire, and I hear his voice. I already memorized everything he had to say, so I'm apt to play it back, filling in the news of the day. The ice broke through the river today, and it's roaring louder than last year, better get some more cordwood in, the stacks getting low, time the mending gets done.

I'm careful, though. I never let him comment on my failings. He wouldn't like the house crowded from stem to stern with wildflowers cut from the field—or a dinner of rice and elderberry jam. I figure it's none of his worry. I make my own choices now.

She Doesn't Get Out of the Airport Much

Not much. Like the spinning of a reel she swirls
passing drinks to folks in a hurry
waiting endlessly

in artificial air. It's nearly a meditation.
She pokes me with a half smile
born of ranchers

and lean cowboys. Points out The Salt Lick,
sticky barbeque. Country cooking
at the airport.

My feet hurt, my bags are heavy. I want a couch
to rest them on. She waltzes by
with a few beers

dancing a bit of a two step to the airport
speakers. The live band tunes up. Texas Country.
Grins all round.

Boarding calls & the TSA grow faint. The music
is so alive we could be at
home on the range.

Strangers sit together with sunny smiles. Their solitary
suit coats hang at odd angles from chairs,
suddenly abandoned.

—Becky Liestman

Father

He carries

the Culligan tank angled across his back—
making thick clunking music as iron
strikes flesh. He struggles on each cellar
stair—one foot, one foot in alliteration.

He is bringing
soft water to small country farms. What is soft for them is hard
for him. The lead weight above him is obliterating. It
will not curve to him, bend to him, his will—
it stands alone.

The crushing weight,
no, has no conscience. It is concrete in its simplicity,
swish sweat seeking him, pummeling him,
intense, sinking.
How hard can an old heart burn?

The farm dog attacks
his leg. Chews at him. Even weighted down,
he has mastered a sharp kick—the dog retreats. He is bringing
home his paycheck, bringing home his paycheck. His feet
are rubber on the farmhouse stairs.

He does his duty.
He is beyond himself
in the trenches of the Aleutian Islands,
bombed daily and daily.
Liberating Dachau.

Just one speck
in the Allied Forces, going on. Picking
potatoes as a young migrant, school at the wayside,
his body will—not—stop. Tending his family. His body will—
not stop. Do not ask for more.

—Becky Liestman

Grand Mound:
A Prehistoric site on the
Rainy River and
U.S. National Historic Landmark

If a little girl could see
into all those layers of still frozen soil
rich in spirits, pottery and artifacts lying quietly

since the great wall of China
was built, she might be astonished.
One hundred years before Julius Caesar,

the Laurel tribes came together—
came here to the confluence of the Big Fork
and Rainy Rivers to fish sturgeon,

gather ripe blueberries. They came to bury
their dead in the earth of Grand Mound, so large
it is tall, almost 3 stories—so enticing

to a small child, playing alone in an isolated flat land.
Perhaps she can still feel the feasting, the trading,
the ancient drumming ceremonies

as people greet each other after a long winter apart.
Perhaps in the dull heartbeat of the soil
she hears the presence of the old ones

in those long swollen hills, speaking of wind
and all natural things. Maybe those fine grains
of bone bind her very soul

to peacefulness, as her small body completely
loses itself in last year's tall grasses. Near the river
she peers into Canada.

Sap flows freely in the maple trees,
never interrupted
by the invisible thread between nations.

Perhaps the ancient ones hear her presence,
share her story. Perhaps their hands are fragile
in the faint retelling, almost as vapors in the moist air.

—Becky Liestman

Haiku

Cadmium Yellow
Maple, Leafed in fall splendor
Caught My Artist's Eye

Watercolor Sky
Blue Grays Melt into Sumac
Clouds Evaporate

—Kristin M. Arneson

Waiting

Fiction: Virginia Sievers

My name is Amanda Riperos, and I am an old person.

In this waiting room we are all old people, sitting quietly on our chairs and marking time together. Some of us leaf through magazines. Some of us have our eyes on the wall television where the volume is turned low. On the screen a smiling blonde talks to us, peppering her talk with inane little laughs as she tells us about a popular and trendy restaurant we should visit. Some of us close our eyes and doze. I am reading a magazine but I put it down and pick up a newspaper another person has left behind.

When the nurse opens the inner door and walks briskly toward us we look up expectantly. She walks with authority and she looks cross, almost currish. Checking a green file, she struggles to pronounce a name while her eyes impatiently scan the room. A woman nods, gets up slowly from her chair, makes her way to the door and, on the way, tells the nurse how the name should be pronounced. "Broo nin' ski," she says, "not Brou nis' ki." The nurse narrows her eyes and openly frowns at the woman. She doesn't acknowledge the correction. I watch from my chair and think this nurse is rude and insensitive and I wonder if she is controlling. I wonder if she is a Nurse Ratched kind of person.

Sitting beside me an overweight and ill-kept man sighs when his name is not called. He is restless. Unlike most of us, he wants to talk.

"Have you been here long?" he asks.

"Yes, for some time," I reply. The man already knows this.

"I've been here for an hour," he tells me. "It's busy today." He nervously shifts his body in the chair.

"Yes," I agree. I don't extend the conversation. Hopefully, he won't go on with his talk.

Across the room a quiet couple listens. As they sit close, they hold hands. The man looks at his watch and points to it. The woman, eyes twinkling, nods her head as she points to her watch, too. They look at each other knowingly and break into smiles. I watch them with disdain, resenting their closeness and resenting their happiness and I think their private joke is silly. My face is in a frown but I remember that our nurse, our own Nurse Ratched, is a frowner and her frown doesn't become her. I quickly erase mine and purposely look away.

When I scan the headlines in the newspaper there is nothing that interests me. As it slips to my lap my hands idly play with the loose pages.

The outside door opens. A new couple comes into the room. As her partner watches the woman struggles to maneuver her walker through the door. She gets it inside and they both head for two chairs near the check-in counter. The man stops at the counter to write on the patient clipboard and I see that, while he is writing, the woman's eyes fill with tears. Sitting down carefully on one of the chairs she puts her purse on her walker and tries to brush away the tears but they slide down her cheeks. Seeing the tears makes me sad for the woman. I want to walk across the room to offer comfort but, once again, I purposely look away.

Nurse Ratched is back, clutching a red file this time. Her eyes narrow. In her impatient voice she calls out a name. The restless man who waited for an hour gets up quickly and walks fast as he follows the nurse through her door. "Finally," he says loudly.

I try reading the newspaper again, then sit quietly for a long time with the paper on my lap. I am tired but make an effort to sit up tall and straight. Someone turned the television off so the loud steady ticking of the wall clock fills the quiet space.

The inner door opens. "Riperos," Nurse Ratched calls into the quiet as she comes into the room. I don't bother to correct the mispronunciation of my name. I just stand and follow her to the door, walking as fast as I can manage. At best, though, my fast walk is a slow dragging shuffle; a shuffle I own now. Lately it has become an embarrassment. To compensate for my slowness I hold my head high and focus my eyes straight ahead.

It is a struggle to keep up with Nurse Ratched's fast pace. Even though my feet slowly drag, my mind is on fast forward. Hurting truths rush into my head.

I consider them one-by-one.

"So it all comes to this," I think. "It all comes to a once-proud old woman padding along behind an odious nurse like an obedient child. It all comes to this."

"To Nurse Ratched I am only one more mispronounced name. To her I am Amanda Rip'er ose, not Amanda Ri per'ous."

The truths race on. "I am a number. Perhaps today I am number five on her list. She is anxious to be done with me so she can go on to number six."

As we near the inner door the unspeakable real truth comes to me. "She thinks I am a bother."

We walk through the door and I stop. Nurse Ratched goes on, then turns around to wait for me. She doesn't like waiting and gives me her best frown but now it pleases me to annoy her. As I start forward again I slow down my already dragging shuffle and make her wait longer. It is pleasantly satisfying to be a bother.

"Right here in this room," Nurse Ratched instructs crossly, eyeing me with suspicion. At first I pretend not to hear but I follow as she leads me through an open door. Like the restless man, I am tired of waiting. "Finally," I whisper to myself.

Nurse Ratched tells me where to sit. She does her eye thing, purses her lips, and gives me one last once-over. She hesitates and looks me up and down again. "She is trying to decide if I am intact," I think. She makes her decision in my favor, turns quickly, goes out the door and, with an in your face attitude, closes it with more noise than necessary. Her footsteps click as she walks down the long outside hall. As the clicks fade into nothing, I am left alone behind a closed door in a little cubicle of a room.

The new room is still. There are no comforting noises here; no muffled television sounds in the background, no soft rustling of papers, no quiet murmurs of people talking, no dependable ticking of a clock. A hollow lonely silence is in this room. Already, even in a few seconds, the silence rings in my ears and pounds at my aloneness with dogged persistence.

I scrunch down in my chair, listening to the silence and pondering my irrelevance. Tears well up in my eyes and slide down my cheeks, just as the sad lady's tears welled up and slid down her cheeks. I do not try to brush mine away. In this noiseless cubicle of a room where the silence is relentless and where I am all alone, it is strangely comforting to let my tears fall freely. By myself I take my time and quietly cry.

After a while the tears ebb. I feel depleted and empty and know I am finished crying. I sit still in my chair waiting for something to happen. Perhaps there will be approaching footsteps or perhaps there will be a gentle knock on the door. To mark time I count the ticks of an imaginary clock. The something I am waiting for does not happen.

I soon grow weary of counting ticks. Resigned, I sigh and settle in and contemplate filling the time space ahead. I think it will be another long wait for one Amanda Riperos (Ri per'ous), an old person.

Sense of Place

I'm searching for a lonely place,
a rusty gent with window sills
like frayed french cuffs,
a roof of mossy cedar shakes
a bit askew, a bad toupee,
and knotty floors needing polish
like scuffed wingtips,
twice, three times resoled.

I'd shine it up with lemon oil
and limed whitewash,
and jars and jars of elbow grease.
I'd settle in, inhale the clean,
sharp, tangy scents,
breathe out, "I'm home!"

A lonesome place is what I'd like,
an aging gal with porch steps sprung
like knees that bounced
a dozen babes, a sagging swing,
her stretch-marked lap,
where someone rocked to dreams
a played out, splayed out child,
a milk and cookies breather.

A pinch or two of chubby cheeks,
ears tuned to swing song lullaby
would cheer it up.
I'd listen to it creak and groan,
and whisper, "House,
you're not alone."

—Bethany Hammer

Hanging Onto Ghosts

By ghosts,
I really mean memories.

I mean specters that cloud my mind,
and leave me stuck in the moments

     I cannot seem to leave behind.

Faint whispers speak,
leading me backwards,

     leaving my thoughts fixed in the past.

     It's a loop,
     a circle,
          an endless flow of repetitive images and words.

How to do I move on,
when the story
     never ends?

Face after face keep flashing.

Voice after voice keep speaking,
and there seems to be no end to the conversation.

All I want is blindness,
        deafness,
        stillness.
Turn,
 "The End"
   turn,
     and the emptiness of a white page.

—B.D. Smith

Aunt Mickey's Rhubarb

Creative Nonfiction: Mike Lein

It had been a tough spring for our old rhubarb plant. First the warm weather of March coaxed it into peeking above the garden mulch way too early. Then the predictable April cold snap froze those tender young shoots back to ground level. That hadn't worried me too much. Rhubarb is a hardy plant and this particular one had been around awhile.

My Aunt Mickey had dug the plant from her western Minnesota garden close to thirty years ago and presented it to us. I don't remember the specific reason. It might have been a house warming gift or she simply might have thought that any young Scandinavian couple should have a rhubarb plant in their garden. But now the plant had been hacked to pieces by my wife in a gardening frenzy while I was off on a fishing trip. One small portion had been transplanted to a planter on the edge of the garden. Most of the rest lay shriveled and dying in the compost pile.

Marcie was unrepentant. "It was in the wrong spot—it had to go! Besides, it will be fine – you can't kill that rhubarb!" Behind her stood my oldest sister, one of her best friends, mortified at what had happened. She was clutching a small remnant of the plant, a sad and wilted fragment, salvaged from the compost.

"I'll take this one home and find a spot for it," she said, clearly understanding the history and family ties to butchered plant and the severity of the offense.

Since the deed had been done, I decided to make the best of it and keep quiet for the time being. Once the women left, I clandestinely salvaged the hacked up pieces from the compost pile and planted the half a dozen small clumps on the out lot behind our garden fence. I didn't need that many rhubarb plants but I couldn't see letting it go to waste. Within the week, two more shoots poked through in the location of the old plant and were quickly moved before Marcie spotted them. And then I found two more somehow clinging to life in the compost pile. So, I ended up with a new 15 foot row of rhubarb in addition to the new old plant, which actually seemed to be doing fine. I added a little fertilizer and mulch to the transplants and waited to see what would happen.

My curiosity led me to doing a little internet research while I waited. As usual, once you start on the internet, one thing leads to another. Like the history of rhubarb. I had always assumed that it was a northern European plant, perhaps a native Scandinavian, cultivated simply because nothing else would grow in frost plagued soil. Wrong, at least according to the wiseness of the internet. Seems like it probably originated in the Far East and slowly traveled westward along the trade routes. The internet also alternatively warned of the toxic nature of its leaves and praised its long known medicinal properties. An ancient Chinese cure for cancer? A little known

Viking love potent? Nope—supposedly the leaves are a great laxative if used in the right amount. Personally, this is one organic herbal "cure" I won't be trying at home.

I also assumed that it was something reserved for pies, deserts, homemade wine, and other sweet delights. Wrong again. According to the Foodie websites, it appears there was a rhubarb revelation several years ago—rhubarb and fish were apparently at least a minor craze. Somehow I had missed that in spite of many hours spent watching cooking and gardening shows during the winter. But since I am always looking for new twists on fish, I gave the rhubarb sauce for fish a try.

Many websites offered up the same generic recipe with only minor variations. So I came up with my own take based on what was available. I bought a small bunch of de-leafed reddish-green stalks at the Chaska Farmers Market since my own plants needed to recuperate before harvesting. Yes, I paid for rhubarb. That has to be a major sin in Scandinavian culture. I am sure Aunt Mickey would have had something to say about that.

I chopped up a couple stalks of rhubarb, a carrot, a shallot, and an onion, and sautéed the mix in butter. I then added white wine and clam juice and simmered it a bit before blending everything to "smooth" in my food processor. The result was a creamy light orange colored sauce with a definite tang. It was a nice compliment to a piece of grilled salmon. Think for a minute—it makes sense. What other seasoning do you use on fish to enhance the flavor? Maybe some sour lemon juice? Think of rhubarb sauce in the same way—something to add a tart spark to fish.

As for other more traditional rhubarb recipes, there's no need for experimentation as far as I am concerned. Just consult the real experts. I just reach for one of the many church fundraiser cookbooks on my kitchen shelf. Trust me here on two things. There will be a rhubarb section, and you can't go wrong with a church lady recipe. I used the rest of my "boughten" rhubarb on a rhubarb coffee cake recipe from one of them. It passed the test at work. The entire pan disappeared from the break room table by noon.

It does look like I am going to need plenty of recipes. Every one of the clones that resulted from Marcie's garden hack job appears to be thriving and ready to produce a bumper crop. Maybe she is right for once. You really can't kill Aunt Mickey's rhubarb.

Fish Sauce Recipe

Finely chopped rhubarb—about a cup and a half
One small carrot—chopped
One shallot—chopped
One medium onion chopped
One tablespoon of unsalted butter
Half a cup of white wine
One cup clam juice

Sauté rhubarb and veggies in butter at low heat until soft [10 minutes]. Add the wine and clam juice. Simmer for 15 minutes. Blend smooth in food processor. Reheat at low temperature and spoon over grilled or baked fish.

The Afghans

One sister asked for sunshine, fire and
blood
Another wanted lilac, leaf and leopard's
eyes
The third asked for silver stones and
ladybug's wings

When it was my turn, I said
"Give me velvet to hang the clouds
on,
Where the plates of stars are set."

And Grandma knitted me
Lake Michigan

—Sue Kunitz

This Day

All suns and moons run to
This day
Frost covers the belly of the earth
Trees undress
As they catch the sun
This day
Outside the door
Pounds
This day hunts for us
Through rivers and streams
This day
Though winter holds it
In its mouth
Roars

—Sue Kunitz

("This Day" was previously published in the Dec. 2005 issue of The Pen Woman under the title "A Day in Winter's Mouth.)

This Day Comes

Howling, This day comes,
Dragging the corpse,
Of yesterday by the hair.
Not mindful of oncoming cars,
Yesterday ran in the street,
Went with the nice man,
And ended up dead.
Yesterday drained the blood from the
Flesh of this new day

—Sue Kunitz

Honey Locust Mom

Yellow bodied,
Black winged,
Sitting on bare branches
Small birds pause
Large crows fly by
All are frightened away

One bird, returns,
Makes the honey locust tree his
Own
He gazes around, then lays
On a branch

His bed, moving branches gently,
Supports the small body so it does
Not fall,
Wraps him in lush leaves,
And attains a beauty
Only the small
Sleeping bird can give.

—Sue Kunitz

The Greatest Man I Ever Knew

Creative Nonfiction: Dale A. Swanson

I took each of the worn pine steps leading to our basement carefully and slowly, finally stopping at the point where he became visible through the open sides, and planted my rear end. I was nine. Moments earlier my mother's message was, "Your father wants to see you."

He was in his small work area, hardly large enough to call a shop, working on a contraption that looked like a nightmare of black metal needles, ends hooked, and situated vertically on the outside of a black cylinder. There was a crank on one side, function unknown to me. He spoke without looking up from his work.

"I heard you and Larry were yelling unkind remarks at Mr. and Mrs. Wilson. Is it true?"

My breathing became ragged. How did he know? It couldn't have been ten minutes since we'd flung insults at the aging couple from behind Johnnies garage; loudly shouted words that to a nine year old were clever and daring.

"DRUNKARD. Have another beer. DRUNKARD, DRUNKARD."

The old man was attempting to back into his driveway,

which was straight as a plumb line, but he couldn't seem to hit it at the right angle, getting out and walking unsteadily to the rear every so often to learn he failed; returning just as unsteadily to try it again. Mrs. Wilson, oblivious, sat in the passenger seat. After about four attempts, we started our chants.

My father, at last, turned away from his work and approached the stairs. Placing his hand on one of the steps, he looked directly into my eyes waiting for an answer.

Tears began to well. "Yeah dad, we did."

"How do you suppose that made them feel?'

Now the crying began in earnest. I was filled with remorse, not for what we had done, but because I had disappointed my dad.

I wanted to be like him. He was Santa Claus at the Island Park community Christmas party. He called Bingo at the annual Fireman's Field Days. He was the scoutmaster for Troop 201 before and after I was old enough to join. And he always had time for me. He proudly went to work each day as custodian at Shirley Hills Elementary School, and he gave us everything we needed.

His discipline was a look, a softly spoken question, a whispered promise to teach right from wrong through example, and deep respect for others. I hope I learned.

I still have the sock-knitting machine he worked on that day.

Haiku

Friary Garden
Summer, noon Sunshine, music
Flowers meditate

Walking the Trail
Cattails and Elderberries
Wild flowers in Fog

—Kristen Arneson

Minnesota Summer Squall

Have you made note of the smell of summer?
Dust invades your nostrils as you stroll
through the August heat.

Overripe pollen of oak, maple and ash
fills your eyes, and you rub seeking to abate the itch
to no avail.

The heat mirage drifts above the tarmac
and the distant clouds are Himalayan peaks.

Sweat drips from your chin while
the unmistakable lake bouquet permeates like
the rich odors of a Turkish kiosk.

The mountains approach with jagged ribbons
as thunder shakes the ground and birds flee

as God dumps a bucket of water
on the parched earth, beating down the pollen
and tarmac image.

Trees drip with the pitter-patter of the deluge past
while the senses fill with the sweet fragrance of alfalfa,
and the corn grows so fast you can hear it.

Immersion in the perfume of fresh earth, washed leaves;
alive in the symphony played by rejuvenated swamps and
lakes.

Have you made note of the smell of summer?

—Dale A. Swanson

Discord

We chop the veggies, stir the dip
put frozen chicken wings on the warped
cookie sheet.

> he perches precariously—

We set the oven to 425.
Seems we've got plenty.
Not so many invited today.

> he bellows his useless air at the foothills, the sky

We watch the games, check our iPhones.
Text our rage at the referee.

> it's no mirage
> his son is missing in action

The buzz of the announcer gets annoying.

> his sound takes the shape of a hollow horror

The crackle of helmets is just what fans like.
A cavernous sound, it roils the country with its
bewitching, stinging power.

his broken finger arches, points to them

We hear Time Expired.

whether a healing balm or torment his life will
seep into theirs

—Becky Liestman

Legions

Fiction: Dale A. Swanson

Funny. It was natural to see his father flying alongside the path, seeming to guide him along his way. Although he had never before seen the others he felt a kinship that came from deep within.

They flitted left and right all the while close enough to touch, guiding him and protecting him. His footsteps, closer together than normal were unfaltering as he trudged toward the crest where he knew the trail curved left before starting its decline.

His father flew to within inches of his right ear, "Come on Son, this couldn't be easier."

He thought of his wife of fifty-seven years and her admonishment for his increased girth. Exercise, she told him. Mild exercise. Perhaps a walk around the lake three times a week, nothing too demanding, but something, anything to interrupt his sedentary lifestyle.

This was his first time and although he thrived on heat, he began to think it was a mistake to start his new regimen during midday under a blazing sun.

Almost from the outset, he saw the dragonflies alongside the paved trail. They hovered, darted ahead only to land on a single blade of grass and wait until he drew even then again raise into the air to repeat the process. As his arms swung to the cadence of his footsteps his mind found refuge in the peace and solitude that enveloped him when he was alone with nature.

He marched along the path, certain that a brisk pace would accelerate the removal of his excess pounds. He thought it odd he felt no sweat on his forehead and that his forearms were absolutely dry. Stranger yet was the formation of his accompanying dragonflies. They now numbered in the hundreds and they were definitely accompanying him on his walk.

He thought "Legions. How strange. It seems you are actually guiding me."

The answer came the instant his thought concluded.

"Your childhood awaits and all you cherished then - will be yours again." As he listened to the wing beats, he began to recognize individuals as they flitted in and out of his vision. There was his father, his mother, gesturing him forward. He saw his grandfather, grandmother, aunts, and uncles all beckoning to him, all darting thither, and yon. How wonderful he thought. How marvelous. What beautiful wings. How safe.

The man in the paramedic uniform knelt by the prone body. "He's gone. Crazy to be walking in this stifling heat."

His partner standing on the other side of the body stared at the inert figure. "It almost seems he's smiling."

Haiku

Night Winds Settle Down
As the Hunter's Moon Rises
All Shadows are still

Swaying on a Reed
The Startled Black Redwing Trills
I will Return Soon

—Kristen Arneson

"Merry Christmas:" An Offense to American Liberty?

Creative Nonfiction: David J. Gollin

It was an unseasonable warm Wisconsin winter day, a few degrees above zero. The sky was overcast and a cold wind blew from the north. A week before Christmas and I was feeling refreshed by the breeze and in the Christmas spirit: at peace with my surroundings and myself.

I pulled open the heavy glass door and entering the vestibule, pausing to listen to the blustery wind and its promise of snow. Opening the second glass door I entered the bank and recognized the smiling faces. After living in the same community for fifteen months I had built casual relationships with people working in the places I frequented. These acquaintanceships gave warmth through the comfort of familiarity.

I filled out my withdrawal slip, approached the counter and went directly to the smiling teller. Another teller, a woman with long dark-brown hair stood with her back to us at the drive-up window.

After completing my transaction I said, "Merry Christmas."

The brunette turned with a scowl and in an angry tone blurted out, "Happy Holidays!"

I was surprised by the vehemence of her reaction and started wondering about the meaning of "Happy Holidays." So I began a brief investigation in order to answer the question: "What is a holiday?"

I went to the Miriam-Webster on-line dictionary (www.merriam-webster.com/dictionary/holiday) and found the following definition:

1: holy day

2: a day on which one is exempt from work; *specifically*: a day marked by a general suspension of work in commemoration of an event

3: *chiefly British*: vacation—often used in the phrase on holiday—often used in plural

4: a period of exemption or relief <corporations enjoying a tax *holiday*>

I am confident that people who insist on the term, "Happy Holiday" are not using the word in the first meaning above, but in the first half of second meaning, "a day on which one is exempt from work; specifically: a day marked by a general suspension of work" but they eliminate the second half of the definition, "in commemoration of an event" since the only event intended from the statement "Happy Holidays" is the amorphous event, time-off. The third definition describing a British vacation, as "on holiday" may be closer to what people mean, but this refers to an individual on vacation, not a societal event.

So definition number two is most applicable. The second question then becomes: "How did this time-off originally come about and what was it intended to commemorate?"

Federal holidays are designated by Congress in Title V of the United States Code (5 U.S.C. § 6103). There are ten such annual holidays, or days when federal employees do not have to report to work. This practice, for most of the ten holidays, is followed by state and local governments as well as by many businesses. Note that in line with definition number two, each holiday commemorates a specific event. Just as Martin Luther King Day was enacted to commemorate the birth of this epic civil rights leader, the Christmas holiday was enacted to celebrate the birth of Jesus Christ. And just as it would seem ridiculous to insist on saying "Happy Holiday" for time off as a result of Martin Luther King's birth it is also nonsensical to say "Happy Holiday" for time off as a result of Christ's birth

"Merry Christmas" means be merry, joyful and exceedingly happy because of the birth of Christ. And Happy Holidays, as used in American culture, means nothing. It is not a sensible greeting since it does not commemorate anything in particular except time-off from work. In fact this statement, "Happy Holidays," is redundant, it is like saying "Happy time-off in commemoration of time-off." I suggest to the politically correct among us that it would make more sense to use either, "Happy Vacation" or "Happy Time-Off."

A sensible compromise, whether we care about Christ or not, might be to simply state, "Happy Christmas Holiday" or "Happy Christian Holiday" meaning we should be happy our founders and some crazy people in Congress chose to influence our whole society by giving us time-off to commemorate Christ's birth. Then we can be true to the meaning of the word, holiday, and when we speak this new salutation we can intend it to imply either a holy day, or to declare time-off and simply be thankful that someone thought celebration of the birth of Christ worth taking off time from our daily grind.

So to all those offended by the salutation, "Merry Christmas" I leave you with the valediction: Have a very merry, joyful and bright time without needing to go to your job and remember, you get this time-off because of those crazy guys in the Congress of the United States of America who had the desire to commemorate the birth of Christ.

Happy Christian Holiday and oh yeah, Merry Christmas!

K.D.

K.D. Your voice swallowed me whole.

Sitting in this old car with your old music,
working its way inside through paths of magic.

The swoon of your vocal cords is
      a sweet drug,
making my head swim the river,
unwinding my thoughts like
      a ball of yarn.

The afternoon heat burns through
      the car window.

Leaning my seat back,
I let those precious words float.

"This tiny lifeboat can keep me dry,
      but my weight is all that it can stand."*

Your old addiction is mine as well.

We've smoked all those smokes, sung all those songs.

My eyes remain closed to the world outside.

All I can hear is the soothing melody of your voice,
wafting through the midday air;
pouring into my waiting ears.

—B.D. Smith

* (Quotation from K.D. Lang's song My Old Addiction)

Swimming

Creative Nonfiction: S.C. Bresson

Hearing stories of others growing up got me thinking of my childhood and a few memories of my own. I remember when I was six living on a farm with my sister and four older brothers. We lived on a place south of Minneota, MN. Mom always found farm places to rent and we ran wild.

The farm had a big house, a hen house, hay barn, and a couple of other buildings. My sister Sue and I would play outside all the time. We made up games to play. Mostly we played horses. Sue and I loved horses, were in fact wild about them. We would whinny, trot, and gallop around the yard. My favorite color for a horse was black and I think I remembered Sue liked white horses. We kept asking Mom to get us a horse, but of course as a single mother with six kids to raise she couldn't. She did it all on her own as my biological father is what is known as a deadbeat dad today. He never sent any money to Mom to help with food, rent, or clothes. We never seemed to notice this lack except when food was short, which wasn't too often with Mom always putting in a huge garden in the summer.

Mom would plant tomatoes, potatoes, cucumbers, peas, sweet corn, radishes, lettuce, green beans, and beets. She would can the tomatoes and green beans, pickle the beets and use the beet juice to make jelly. I didn't like pickled beets when I was young and I still don't, but the jelly was delicious!

Summer was a time of exploring. Sue and I would trail after my brothers closest in age to us, Mark and David. We would explore the pasture behind our house. We would follow Mark and David even though I'm sure they told us to stay home. The pasture had cows in it and while we weren't scared of them we did keep away. I don't recall if it was anything my oldest brother Loren said or because Mark and David had a healthy respect for them. We just followed what they did. Which also meant not stepping in any cow pies! Yuk!

We had fun throwing rocks in the shallow creek and teasing snapping turtles as well as catching mud turtles. With the snappers we made sure we had long and very strong sticks. The snappers would indeed snap at them and Sue and I would drop our sticks and run screaming away, only to come back and watch David and Mark continue the game until the snapper finally escaped into the stream.

I never had swimming lessons. Sue and I learned to swim in the pasture water. We stayed near the shallow part of the creek. I remember the water as being so clear I could see to bottom. The water ran lazily over the stones lying on the creek bed. I don't remember being afraid of jumping into the water, dunking under with eyes open and swimming under for as long as I could hold my breath. It felt like I was in another world. The sun so bright the water seemed yellow to my eyes as I swam.

When we went swimming we had a routine. After the first time swimming in that water we brought not just our towels, but also a saltshaker filled to the brim. Why the salt? Well, swimming the creek and getting out we had passengers attached to us, mostly between our toes. Leeches. I have a vague recollection of David and Mark laughing at me the first time leeches sucked from my limbs. They slapped our hands and showed Sue and I how to get rid of them the proper way. You never pulled leeches off—just salted them and they fell off. After that first time I wasn't squeamish about those critters. Now I wouldn't touch them with a ten-foot pole!

Oh yeah, the turtles we caught. We always let them go after we were done playing with them before went home.

Vanishing

Diminishing, reducing, shrinking
Disappearing, dying, vanishing
Heartbeat slowing, slower, almost gone
Smaller, smaller
Pillaged, ravaged, subdivided, fertile land, gone
Heritage sold, going broke, no way out
Families leaving, heartbroken, some forced by city and county
Waves of grain a memory, hurting
Cookie cutter houses, small yards, encroaching
All the same, no beauty, crowding, crowding, need more room!
Where will our food come from?
Who will be left to grow it?
Where are those small town values?
Progress they say, people need a place to live
Diminishing, disappearing, vanishing,
The American farm.

—S.C. Bresson

Spring Cleaning

Spring sprang cleaning
    on the snoozing woods.

Puffs of whisking wind
    buffed snow drops off
their silver birch perch.
    flung them off the limp,
      stippled limbs
like cotton rag mops pop fluffy,
    scruffy dust bunnies
out from under antique bedsteads,
    feathered Bird's Nest quilts,
      eyelet skirts.
Brisk breezes swept, prepped
    the tree house, aired out
the warbler inn; chinook shook boughs.
    Ice, not dust motes floated,
      coated the ground.

Woods stood waiting
    for the nesting guests.

—Bethany Hammer

Avuncularities

Fiction: D. E. Munson

For over a year I'd bugged Uncle Jesse for the large-print King James bible he promised. Poor guy, I was merciless. But in the end, he came through, and I cherish that book to this day.

Uncle Jesse was an interesting character. Descended of the infamous Jesse James, he deserves note for posterity. I recently started fantasizing he was ol' Jesse-come-back-around to atone.

Though he was born and raised in Iowa, he began his ministry in tiny Fenton, New York. He was a bachelor when he'd arrived there, but didn't stay that way for long. He captured the heart of the sweet, dark-curly-haired girl in the congregation who became my Auntie Mercy.

Even as a young man he was not quite slim, but the years brought him girth. He had a presence.

They married shortly after the end of World War II, then moved to Uncle Jesse's native Iowa. They stepped into the 1950s adopting my girl-cousins, Jay and Kay. They remained in Iowa until the 1960s and the coming of the Kennedy's. Much of the world's attention, as well as the James family, was drawn to New England.

Uncle Jesse's new parish was to be at the Allen Street Methodist Church in New Bedford, Massachusetts. While I was busy extolling the virtues of Richard Nixon to Mom and Dad in 1960, Auntie Mercy was busy shaking Jack Kennedy's hand. I'm grateful that God works in mysterious ways or the sixties might've been a different story.

New Bedford, home of Captain Ahab, would become one of our favorite vacation spots for years, formative years, to come. In 1962, just before we set out on such a vacation, Uncle Jesse and the James family visited us. That was when we'd just moved into our white, Cape Cod-style house on Echo Road in Vestal, New York. Late one sunny morning, Uncle Jesse paid me, in my mind, the ultimate compliment at the time.

Frodo's big brother Dillon had just bequeathed me the tail section of a big red and black model plane he'd crashed. He was about to pitch it, but I blurted, "I'll take it!"

"Okay, but it's just junk," he replied.

"I know, but it's cool." My junk-collecting tendency still haunts me.

* * *

Anyway, I bounded into the kitchen with my new prize. Uncle Jesse sat chatting with Dad at the Formica table, but the slam of the screen door snapped his attention in my direction.

"What do ya have there?" he queried.

"Oh, it's the rudder and stabilizer from a model plane. A friend of mine just gave it to me."

His eyes lit with curiosity. "What did you call that? The second thing?"

"The stabilizer?"

"Yes, that's it," he nodded. "The stabilizer. Tell me about this stabilizer. What does it do?"

"Well, it helps the plane keep flying straight. The pilot uses it to control the up and down movement of the plane."

"Is that so?" he replied, stroking his chin.

"Would you mind if I borrowed it for a little while? I think I'd like to use it in my children's sermon Sunday."

I hesitated, fearing the loss of my newfound treasure. Then I remembered we were all about to caravan to New Bedford for our vacation. I relented with the thought, *I'm actually helping Uncle Jesse prepare his sermon.*

Three days later I sat in a back pew of the church with the family. Uncle Jesse stepped up and stood beside the pulpit. I felt giddy.

"How many model airplane enthusiasts do we have here?" he asked the congregation. A smattering of hands went up. Uncle Jesse reached over to the top of the pulpit.

"Does anyone know what this is?" A little rustling in the pews was the only response. "I couldn't have guessed what it was, either. But my nephew tells me this is a piece of a model airplane called the stabilizer." I was beaming.

Uncle Jesse continued, "He explained how the stabilizer helps an airplane fly straight and true. It came to me that we, each of us, can use one of these.

"If we imagined we were like that airplane, and that the air we fly through is life, you could say God is our stabilizer.

"Say we're tempted to say or do something that makes us feel good in the moment. Now, suppose a little voice inside tells us it will pull us down or hurt somebody else. When we don't listen to that voice, the stabilizer loses control, and we get pulled down.

"I know this is easier said than done, but if we just remember this little stabilizer, we can fly straight and true and be happier as we fly through life."

"Amen," I chuckled.

* * *

Our New England vacations were magical. They were part Kennedy magnetism and part historical connection. It was easy to feel closer to the Creator as I stood on the shore contemplating the ocean's vastness. I'd sit on the sand at Horseneck Beach savoring a pint of fried clams, listening to the seagulls cry and the roaring surf. I watched wave after wave spend its energy on the beach.

I would daydream about the past and scenes from J. M. Barrie's The Little Minister, my favorite book at the time. I had no idea it was by the same author as Peter Pan. I daydreamed about the future, about helping people in my parish, and about standing at the pulpit. My time hanging around the pulpit then only consisted of being an altar boy.

I loved donning the robe and striding to the altar. With decorum and the twin-tipped golden lance, I'd touch the flaming wick to the candles before the service. With equal relish I snuffed them with the lance's golden bell after service's end. I savored my weekly fix at the altar during that thirty seconds to a minute. I could see, out of the corner of my eye, what the congregation looked like from up front.

* * *

The most important moment in all my sixteen years on the planet culminated at that same pulpit. Reverend Creighton pinned the God and Country medal to my Scout uniform. The feeling I got when the congregation applauded my achievement could become addictive. A dangerous prospect for an Aries trying to be humble.

While becoming an Eagle Scout was the brass ring on the Boy Scout merry-go-round, mine was the God and Country award. I studied and worked hard for it. I did community service and volunteered in the church office for a year. I licked, stuffed, and stamped thousands of envelopes. I also typed labels and glued them to tithing boxes, all on a small table underneath a framed print of Walter Sallman's *Christ at Heart's Door*.

The Beatles were in full swing by then. George Harrison began looking East and studying sitar under Ravi Shankar. I got permission from Miss Husong to set up a portable phonograph to play a Ravi Shankar album as I worked. Thinking back, that was the first seed to bloom into my theological change of direction a few years later.

* * *

My first time at the pulpit came when I was to announce the church White Elephant Sale. I couldn't be satisfied with just reading the announcement from the church program. Nooo, I had to improvise. I stood, both hands gripping the pulpit, surprised to feel a flutter of nervousness when I opened my mouth.

"Ladies and Gentlemen," I announced. "I'm privileged to invite you to the big White Elephant Sale. It's next Saturday in the church basement from ten a.m. to three p.m." I felt the attention and energy of the congregation. "So bring your elephants, white, pink, grey, or otherwise, with or without sneakers to this gala event. You won't want to miss it!"

I've felt little more gratifying than the surprised laughter from those gathered before me. Reverend Creighton shook his head, but was still smiling when he reclaimed the pulpit.

* * *

Now, back to the beach.

I'd just finished my fried clams when I noticed brother Bryan beginning construction of a sand castle. I busted out of my reverie and joined in manifesting Camelot. Bucket by bucket, we excavated the moat. Bucket by bucket, the walls arose and the turrets arose.

As the shadows lengthened and the sun lowered toward the horizon, the sea breeze carried a slight chill. The walls and turrets had grown to shoulder height while we were on hands and knees. All too soon Auntie Mercy came by to admire our handiwork.

"That's wonderful, boys. It's so big. But it's time to go soon. Why don't you run down and wash off the sand."

We set out for Cape Cod after breakfast the next morning. Bryan, three-year-old Esther, and I wanted to ride with Grandpa and Grandma Mac in their green Nash Rambler. Mom, Dad, Elizabeth, and the cousins rode in our white Ford station wagon with imitation Woody panels decorating the doors.

The drive seemed forever, but by midmorning we arrived at Hyannis Port. Grandma and Grandpa ooo'd and ahh'd at the quaint and resplendent cottages. I was digging it. Bryan could've cared less, and Esther was squirmy.

"I ga to pee!"

"Okay, Esther," said Gramma. "We'll look for a gas station or a good place to pull over."

"I got go now!" Esther cried, her face flushing, eyes filling with tears.

"Pull over, Roy," Gram ordered.

"But . . ."

"Pull over now. This child is hurting."

Obliging, Grandpa pulled over in front of a large, stately, white Cape Cod house with a long driveway. In a flash, Grandma was out of her passenger side door, escorting Esther out the rear door (kept open for privacy). Poor Esther was finally able to relieve herself in a Maxwell House coffee can. Good to the last drop.

A hefty security guard approached us, face krinkled like he was holding back a smile. He addressed this novel situation, "What's going on here, folks?" He asked in as official a voice as he could muster.

"She had to go . . ."

"Do you realize you are on the front lawn of the Kennedy's summer home?"

"Oh my. Oh no . . ."

Back on the couch with my box of treasure and pain I whispered to myself, "Thus concludes our personal brush with Camelot."

An excerpt from D. E. Munson's newest novel *In Search of Space & Thyme*

The Winters, the Outsiders

Some are born in it,
Others are born as it

The gentle ferocity, admirable
The vicious reliability, observable

The razing race of something-bent winds
Alongside the caressing touch of air

This is the winter which the natives choose
To either embrace or to distaste

Because not everyone can appreciate naturally,
Or find a way to like it anyway

This is the winter existence for whom some are chosen
A deep, frozen, intricate wonder, met with embrace or distaste

Because not all can have a feel for the difference
Or find a way to see the beauty

Winter, a lovely, difficult, rich, boundless season
A season to live in or a season for life

—Christopher Lemke

Poetic Nuts

Writing a poem is like
taking an oak tree, all
its branches, its rough
bark, even its fat trunk—
the leaves fresh and green
and red ones, too; take
some of the gold leaves
to add richness and brown
for crackle and crunch—
take the whole tree and
tuck it all back into an acorn.
Keep that acorn in a pocket—
in your head. You will need
a nut someday when the sun
shines and you feel like your
hair is burning and your feet
are hot from the pavement.
Then you can open that acorn, take
that tree back out, bit by bit.
Relax in the coolness of it
listen to the leaves sighing
relieved to be free to sway
and dance in fresh air. Watch
the roots dig deep into your
thoughts and grow some more.

Yes, writing a poem is a lot like that.   —A. Carol Scott

Coward

Fiction: S. Collin Ellsworth

Ada speeds down County Road Twenty Four. She is going eighty miles per hour. The speed limit is forty five. She knows she is being reckless, yet she has no choice. Her supervisor told her she was on her way to the third strike. Arriving one minute late means termination.

There is only one job in Small County that pays a decent enough wage so one doesn't have to have multiple jobs. The Metal Factory didn't have many jobs where a woman could meet the requirements. It was back breaking work. If it didn't have stable morning hours, she wouldn't have applied. She can only trust her teenage sister to care for her kids before school. After school, the ungrateful brat ditches the kids so she can make out with her boyfriend.

Ali, that brat. She's the reason Ada is running late. Ali waltzed into Ada's apartment thirty minutes late not caring to leave her boyfriend's trailer five minutes early. Ada doesn't know why her mother lets sixteen year old Ali date a twenty one year old. At Ali's age, a five year gap matters....It's seven forty five, she only has five minutes to clock in! She steps on the gas.

The open country road is endless field. Driving on it

makes a mind wonder. Ada's mind wonders to the bills she has to pay.

Is there one she can miss without the creditors noticing? Her ex hasn't paid child support in six months. He quits his job whenever the state garnishes his wages. Ada doesn't dare ask her mom again. She only reminds her that she has her own child to care for. That damn Ali....

It's a second she can't register. His entire length bouncing off of her windshield and the bumper onto his mailbox. The car's vibrations jolt her body as the impact finally catches to her eardrums. She looks in her rearview. He lays motionless on the ground.

"Oh My GOD!"

Ada glues her eyes to the rearview. In her head she wills him, "Get up! Get UP!"

He doesn't.

Ada's heart pleads with her to stop and get out of the car. She needs to check if he is injured. She needs to call the police.

Ada's brain urges her to step on the gas.

"I'll call the cops after I clock in. I'll clock in and go to the bathroom. I'll call the cops then. I can leave an anonymous tip."

She'll be at the factory in three minutes...

It only takes one second for the mind to spiral. In a minute a mind can completely change.

"The police will wonder how I know about the hit. They will wonder why I didn't stop to check if he was okay. What if he's hurt and the police figure out I hit him? What if they arrest me?"

Ada can't be arrested. Her mother isn't fit to supervise her children. She fell off the wagon a month ago. She drinks while Ali runs around with boys too old for her. Aside from her mother and Ali, Ada has no one nearby to help. Her children will have to go to foster care!

"I can't let that happen!"

Ada wants to do the right thing, but not at the expense of her babies. She can't do that to her babies. She has a daughter. Ada knows from experience that girls don't fare well in the foster system.

"Someone will see him on the road," Ada tells herself, "Someone will call the police."

"Coward!"

Ada looks into her rearview mirror. There He sits with his lifeless eyes transfixed on the reflection of her eyes. She can see the passing tree at the rearview window through His transparent head. His wrinkled face forms into a sneer.

"Coward."

Ada sees the metal factory ahead and steps on the gas. Co-workers in the parking lot scream obscenities at her as she speeds into her parking spot. She runs out of the car to the office, punching in without a second to spare. Surrounding co-workers start questioning her as she runs to her locker.

"Ada, what the…."

"Ada, where was the fire?"

"Ada, do you realize that you almost killed me out there?"

She ignores everyone as she puts on her Personal Protection Equipment. She goes to her welding station.

When Ada pulls down her facial shield, she see His lifeless eyes in her visor.

Ada runs to the bathroom and splashes cold water on her face. Slowly, she lifts her face from the sink to the bathroom mirror. There He is staring at her through the glass.

"Coward."

"I'm not a coward!" Ada shouts.

He snorts, "Enjoy the hell you created."

He fades away. It won't be the last time Ada sees him. He will always be there any time she has to look at her reflection. This is the hell Ada created for herself on earth.

Dryer

We had so
many
conversations
with the door
shut
We laughed
together every
morning
Your hot
breath lifted
the laundry
room curtains
up
Now you
gallup and
roar
About as
subtle as a
space shuttle
launch
I shut the
door

Silent now
I find myself
wrinkled
Watching
puddles grow
Under the
hanging
clothes
Miss the
vibration of
life
When you
made summer
Doesn't seem
fair does it?
That after
twenty years
You end up in
the junk yard
With your
mouth
hanging open.

—Sue Kunitz

Cry Uncle

Fiction: Brian Busch

As I walked the marble floors and brick-lined hallways of Carrier of the Cross Seminary with Sam Renteria, it was hard for me to believe that Sam had a desire for the priesthood.

Still I wanted to get to know Sam a little better. Sam was the only seminarian besides myself with a family member in the clergy. Reverend Carlo Renteria joined a seminary after Sam's mother died from cancer. I think he really misses his mother. In the first three months here at Carrier, he must have mentioned her twenty times.

"Horton, if you stop in during free time," Sam offered, "I can show you my mp3 collection and we can hang out. I have some two-liters of pop, and Xbox. My roommate is never around, so whaddya say?"

"Sure, Sam, sounds like fun," I replied.

Then Sam looked down a bit, turned and looked around him as if he would reveal a secret. "I can show you some other stuff, too," Sam continued. "Have you ever gotten high before?"

"Ah, no Sam, " I was laughing through my words. "No ...I have not."

I thought he was kidding, but it became apparent that

he wasn't. He stared at me for a long time, then said, "No prob, man. It's easy," he half-chuckled and patted me on the shoulder several times. "I'll see you at 3:30. My dorm, if you forgot, is 104," Sam said as he turned down another hallway. I wasn't going to take him up on his invitation. Instead I went to my dorm to get some more books.

When I arrived, I glanced at my cell phone sitting on my desk. The message indicator icon was showing. I picked up the phone and played the message: My parents wanted me to come home and visit them. I had just seen them last weekend. First thing Saturday morning, I was on the road to Neillsville.

I was raiding the refrigerator in my parents kitchen when my Mom walked in.

"What's up, Mom....so, did you miss me and needed me to come home?" I was grinning but I knew that wasn't the reason.

"Sit down, Michael. We have something to tell you about your father's brother."

"Uncle Richard?" They almost never called Richard "my father's brother."

"Uh, OK," I replied.

My father's brother had been a priest up until about six months ago. I didn't know why he left the priesthood and my parents didn't say why, if they even knew themselves. Uncle Richard received his training at Carrier of the Cross Seminary about twenty years ago.

"We never told you this, but your uncle was...well....he did some immoral things. Now that you are in the seminary, I think you deserve to know..."

"Richard is a homosexual," my father said as he walked in from the garage and stopped to give me a stare, his eyes peering out above the rim of his glasses.

"Dad!"

"He is, at least I sure as heck think he is, but I can't prove it. I never see him."

My mom joined in, saying: 'Ronald, are you sure we should be discussing this with him- now?

"Well, isn't that why he was so hush, hush, about this? Its got to be the reason, Grace. "

"I can't believe I am hearing your father say this," Mom covered her mouth, aghast, and looked right at Dad, who walked past her, then stopped and sighed.

"We feel like its time you knew, Michael," my father continued. "He was defrocked. Your uncle has gotten a little too close to some of the boys at St. Matthias school."

I stood up and said emphatically, 'That's not the uncle I know," and I left the house.

A cool breezy Sunday evening air blew in through the windows of my light blue Ford Sedan, given to me by my uncle, as I pondered what Dad said to me yesterday. I would need to clear my head though, before I reached the seminary.

How can Dad say that about someone from his own family? It was a shock.

When I fell off my bike once, Uncle Richard was visiting the house and he ran to assist me before my parents did. I still remember that. My dad had never had a grudge against Richard but they were never close. Dad was hardworking and dedicated to his family, but my mother once described him as irritable, indecisive and sometimes distant. I didn't have much of a relationship with him. He was the boss; I was the underling. I entered the campus, and my worries were: would he face a court hearing? How would he deal with being accused?

I arrived just in time for mass, but I needed to stop at my dorm and bring in some things Mom had given me. I kept thinking about Father Richard. From my closet I dug out an old picture of Uncle Richard and me at my First Holy Eucharist. I grabbed an empty picture frame from under my bed and slowly put the picture in and set it on my nightstand. I stared at it. I kept staring, and was overcome with emotion, wiping away the wetness in my eyes.

If Dad knew something about his homosexuality before, and he must have known something, why didn't Mom and I know about it? There's no shame in it, just the actions that go along with it, are the sin. I refuse to believe he was defrocked. I had to put my dad's words out of my mind as I got into a prayerful mood for mass.

The late mass on Sunday night was started at Carrier to

accommodate any seminarians who were coming back from visiting their parents for a weekend. Father Brooks wanted the mass, and although it took some extra volunteering on our part, we were happy to serve the Lord twice on two Sundays. All of the administrators kept track of the students that went away for the weekend, so that attendance at that mass could be enforced.

The St Francis Xavier Hall of Nature was a beautiful atrium at the entrance to the church, with red and yellow tulips, and trickling ponds with lily pads, and the sound of life-giving water. Catholic symbolism was abundant. The scene in the flower-filled atrium tonight was not so much a symbol of peace: it was a symbol of chaos.

People milled about, talking loudly. Father Brooks was in the atrium with a group of about ten seminarians and some parents who arrived for mass, so I suspected something was up when I walked in. I've never seen him anywhere except through the glass window of his office.

"Where is Sam Renteria? Mass is about to begin!" He questioned a group who hung out with him. Scott Crenshaw was with him last, but all Scott knew is that he went to his dorm.

"I tried his dorm", Zachary Preston called out. "It's locked." Then Zach began to share some experiences about Sam's battles with depression. Father Brooks, trying to change the subject, interrupted Zach.

"Everyone, go to mass...Father Emmanuel Brooks put

up his hands in disgust and circled around. Suddenly a loud siren broke the air like a gunshot. An ambulance arrived in the parking lot, and they followed it to the eastern part of the campus. More seminarians came out of the pews sensing a problem. In the residence wing, a seminarian ran up and met the group head on, and they all stopped.

"Emergency medical personnel are in Sam Renteria's dorm....right now!" The Seminarian turned and ran toward the residence wing. I followed, saying a silent Hail Mary for Sam. I arrived to a crowd of people. Onlookers jammed the doorway of Renteria's dorm. I pushed my way past a few people. There was a hanging IV tube, some belts and equipment, and a paramedic and an emergency medical technician. I craned my neck, but could not tell if Sam was breathing.

"Please, clear the doorway. Excuse me! Excuse me!" The lead paramedic shouted at people as he attempted to turn the gurney wheels a bit. The five or so people in the doorway fell over each other in an attempt to quickly clear out.

I felt relief as the mask Sam wore turned white from his breath. I thanked the paramedic, stepped away from the bedlam, and followed him a couple of steps down the hallway.

He turned to me, and said, "We're not the first ones to get to him. A bystander provided CPR to the victim before we got here."

"Really?" I asked, gathering myself amid the panic. "Who was the bystander?"

His hands on the gurney, he pointed with a head nod. "Guy in the corner, sitting down".

The crowd was out of the room now. I stopped walking and turned back to look through Sam's door. I could see the back wall and a few guys sitting on Sam's bed. As they stood and slowly filtered away, I could now see the man in the corner: An older gentleman with thinning, gray hair, his head held down, face obscured. The quick-acting, good Samaritan that may have saved Sam's life.

I was thinking of something to say, and then he looked up. It took me just a moment to recognize a face that I have not seen in a long, long time. It was my uncle, Richard Horton.

(This story is an excerpt from Brian's novel-in-progress)

Local Treasure

Bethany Hammer

Rhythmic chomps stop the romping bronze-haired boy who turns, spies a thin lady's fingers clutch a Honeycrisp, a chartreuse fruit brushed pink as amaranth. Called by those who know a fine "hand apple," great for eating, its juicy droplets gloss her lips, scarlet lined, and fingertips.

The cheeky youngster perches on the orchard's wood plank checkout stand and spouts a folksy, "Howdy!" He watches as the grandma from the city nods polite "Hello," her covered mouth a-munch. His mouth, a front tooth missing, waters, wishful of the white gold flesh in candy-red wrapping.

"That's our apple," touts the hovering, green-eyed sprout, a produce patriot, proud of Carver County's prize. "Beats those ones from out of state," drones the budding spokesman, skinned fists firmly planted on slim hips poured in blue jeans handed down, scuffed knees buffed with clover stains.

The tourist, mindful of the child's impassioned buzz, chuckles, holds out a bucket tucked with Honeycrisps, offers him a couple. Flashing back a scampish grin, he mumbles thanks, flies off to share the wealth. Beaming pleasure, the woman turns to go, knowing who, not what, is local treasure.

(Inspired by group exercise at Chanhassen Library's visual poetry workshop.)

Hildy

Creative Nonfiction: Diane Popovich Lynch

She lies on the bed in her short-sleeved sweater, culottes and bare feet. Her arm is resting on her head. Her gray-tinged brown curls fall around her scalp exposing large, hairless, scarred areas resulting from many radiation treatments. Her big blue eyes are closed, sunken within her high, square cheekbones. Her skin has a sallow look to it.

I sit down beside her, like I've done so many times before, touching her thin, frail arm so gently. This is our time together. She loves the attention from me. I gently brush her hair, starting on the left side of her head, moving down slowly with my right hand and lightly touching her hair with my left hand as the brush moves along.

I stroke her hair methodically, ignoring what I can't reach as she lays there. And when I finish, she smiles, faintly, like she has so many times before.

Next I bring out my red manicure set--the one I was given at my confirmation nine years before. Those were the days when manicure sets meant something. The small set had a scissors and a pick and a flat headed implement with a red handle. They all fit neatly into a red leather case. The flat-headed tool was our favorite. With it, I carefully move the body lotion down across my mother's thin arms, one stroke at-a-time, making one long line, carefully scraping the residue and moving it over to a dry area.

Her skin was like Grandpa's—shiny and paper thin—so thin that each vein showed through. I imagine blood pumping through those veins, pouring into areas that would soon collect mutant cells and grow into tumors.

Once I complete moisturizing her arms, I move to her legs. Her short legs are extremely pale and hairless. Her skin is as transparent and smooth as her arms. Working with the small flat-headed implement, it takes a long time to move the lotion back and forth over each leg.

We say very little. After our ritual one day she whispered, "You know, if I leave here again, I will not be coming back." In a naïve and hopeful fashion, I quickly responded, "Don't say that, Mom. Of course you'll be back." But, at some deeper level, I knew what she said was true.

After I am done with the ritual, I notice her breaths are shallow now and each one takes so much energy. I lay down beside her once again, stroking her hair and I close my eyes.

Opening My Eyes

On May 24, you took flight
You didn't ask
We didn't know
That you would leave us so soon.

Wait, not yet...stay...
My words were caught by the wind
And carried by a prayer
As you were swept away.

With you, there were joyous musings
That transformed even the most mundane of life.
A new view—a new world
I breathed them in every time I was with you.

Time is different for me now.
It is memorialized
In the number of years that have passed
Since your 32nd birthday.

Those living years are not really that long ago.
Yet.
I still remember those early years
When we struggled to love each other
As mother and son.

As a young adult, your way of Being
Took ahold of you.
It carried us
To a pinnacle of new understanding.

That was always there
But was hidden by old wounds
And lives lived in two different generations.

Somewhere, in between all the scars,
We reached across the wide chasm,
Grabbed ahold of each other's hands
And clung like acrobats in a grasp of life.

Someplace in our souls
We saw each other
As the spirits we knew we really were.

All the armor we built up in our lifetimes
Dropped away, quickly and noisily at first
Then quietly, as if in slow motion
It all fell away.

So many times in those enriching years
When some new spiritual revelation excited me.
I passed the wisdom onto you
And you quietly acknowledged it.

Sometimes you asked just one question,
"What do YOU think?"
And answering it catapulted my new inspiration
Into grave doubt.

Yes, my son
You were my teacher
I hope I was yours, too,
In some small way.

And as the days and years slip by
My eyes search for glimpses of you
In faces of young men I pass as old as you would be
Now.

But you are not there.
You are here, in my world.
Alive in my wakefulness
And in my sleep.

My teacher, still.

—Diane Popovich Lynch

Strength

Your nonsense feeds my anger with you.
You're frustrated with your burden.
To lighten your load, you throw it at me
Weighting each piece down with Guilt, Pity and Regret.

And, when each piece slams into me,
You wonder, "What strange science is at work?"
Instead of falling to the ground with each collision
I grow taller.

Each missile that is hurled at me
Becomes diminished as it pelts me.
And You
You shrink in size as each finds it mark.

You melt
Until you are only a faint whisper
And you cast
No more shadow.

—Diane Popovich Lynch

Sacred Dance

Fiction: Dan O'Brien

While driving cross-country, as Hank often did to ply his wares, the weight of his eyelids grew stronger than the persistence to drive yet a little further. He'd be home soon enough to craft more items from wood to sell in the five Midwestern states he frequented. He decided to pull into a side town, an oasis along the river in the middle of South Dakota just off of Highway 90.

The bump, bump, bump of the tires grew farther apart as the car slowed down and edged onto the off ramp. Ascending to the stop sign there were two options for hotels, one to the right, the "Travelers Inn" and one to the left, the "Western History Hotel." An interest in history, fostered since grade school, won out. Leftward the car was drawn over a gravel road, wind whistling through the cracked passenger side window. On the right side of the road, the Western History Hotel was sparsely lit under a twilight sky with stars twinkling. Hank pulled into the lot and got out of his car. A cat meowed making him feel more like he was on a farm than at a hotel. The wind buffeted his face both waking him and urging him into the lobby of the hotel manned by Jeffry, the sole owner of the place who stood behind the counter in a cowboy hat rubbing his whiskers.

"Hello, young man. You like history then, do ya?" Jeffrey asked.

"Well, I guess so. Does that mean you have a room for the night? Been drivin' all day and would like to get some shut eye."

"Yep, got a room, so long as you like history."

"I do. Have so since I was a kid."

"Good. Plenty of history here. Just have to keep an eye out for it," Jeffrey said, pointing to the posters of Billy the Kid, the settlers who came west and famous Native Americans such as Crazy Horse or Chief Joseph.

Wanting to admire them more, Hank paid the posted rate of 50 dollars a night and slowly meandered past them toward the back of the building where Jeffry had indicated that his room would be "1876." Upon entering he found a poster of Custer's last stand on the wall by the bed. That, too, had been a conscious choice. He had chosen it over "Wounded Knee" and "The Homestead Act."

Hank settled in and drank a pungent, bitter beer, compliments of the house, though Hank couldn't get Jeffry to divulge the name of the company that made such a dark, full-bodied beer, only muttering, "Been brewin' it for a while now."

Ready to turn in, Hank dressed in his pajamas and turned off the light. No sooner had the light gone out, when two things happened. Second thing first. Hank was drawn to the window in amazement. Since Hank was the last one to have any light on at the hotel, even the entryway lights having been turned off, there was no light aside from the stars for miles, but Hank only recalled this later because something much more pressing had caught his attention, the first thing that had happened.

He had heard drumming, which continued intermittently, just beyond a hill off to the left of his vision in the west, and as his eyes adjusted to the night he realized that there was another light beyond that hill, that of a campfire. He had been to a Wacipi, a communal Native American dance, years before but wondered what would have prompted the local people (he presumed the local tribe) to be having a pow-wow at this time of night on a Sunday. Didn't everyone have to go to work the next day? he wondered. His interest in other cultures was piqued. He wanted to know.

He lay back down on his bed and listened. The drumming continued unabated for ten minutes at which point he could no longer quell his wish to know more. He had to go see what this drumming was all about. He got out of bed, put his jeans and his cowboy boots back on and went out into the hall as quietly as he could. He slipped out the back door, believing that no one had noticed him leaving. To his relief, when he stepped in a puddle, no one could have heard the splash since the drums were deafeningly loud. By and by he was coming up to the hill. He began to climb it.

Cresting the hill he looked down on Native Americans dressed in traditional attire, all circling the fire with steps that demonstrated mastery of the art of dancing and suggested exuberance at the same time. They seemed to be celebrating. Hank was about to climb back down the hill and try to think of a way to join them when that became unnecessary. Two braves grabbed his arms and roughly escorted him down to the fireside. He feared that this wouldn't be the kind of fireside chat that he'd heard about given by President Roosevelt or other presidents.

He'd been made to sit, and the two braves stood over him menacingly. All looked at him as the music for the first time since the lights went out—stopped. He said hello, but no one responded. He tried to speak to tell them he'd been to pow-wows before, but not one of them acknowledged his outburst. It became clear to him that they wished him to be silent. Reluctantly, he complied.

There seemed to be some sort of impromptu council taking place across the campfire from him. The cool breeze at his back sent a chill up his spine. The closeness of the braves, sweating from the dance and revelry made him uneasy. This was a far cry from his hope to join in. He was often a willing participant in celebrations, but was becoming quite concerned. He had had no intention of spoiling the festivities, but clearly had. A couple approached him.

"From where do you come at this time?"

"Ah, I am driving."

"The buffalo away?"

"No. Ah, I am crossing this country."

"A hunter?"

"Well, I enjoy the hunt."

"As all braves do. Are you a scout?"

"I was a scout, but…"

"AAAAAh!" the couple shouted out loud and returned to tell what seemed to be a group of elders the result of their conversation with the young man.

"I am not a scout now," he got out when the brave on his left hit him on the back of his head. He felt compelled to return to a forced silence once again.

"You government?" Hank thought he heard the other brave say under his breath after a several minutes.

"No, I move around the country for work." The other hit both of them back into silence. The couple returned.

"You alone."

"Yes, I'm alone on the plains tonight."

"You married?"

"Yes, my wife is in Minnesota."

"Aah!" they yelled again. Then told him that they had lived in the land called Minnesota until recently but wanted to move around more and not be confined to their small allotment of land so moved west to hunt. Hank imagined being confined to a small reservation in Minnesota. He greatly valued his freedom to roam.

"I enjoy the freedom to move about greatly," he said pensively. He noticed that the couple moved in closer upon hearing this.

"You come to take our freedom? You must be stopped," they said unnervingly close to him now.

"No, I honor your freedom," he got out solemnly, following up with, "as I do mine... and that of all people." They seemed to soften at the word honor, perhaps hearing the sincerity in his voice, though the look on their faces betrayed confusion. He wondered if they had trouble understanding his English. He was amazed that in the twenty-first century it was a challenge to understand his words.

"Wait here," they commanded. The two braves looked intensely back and forth from Hank to the couple, but did not intervene. The couple returned to the council once more. After hearing their rendition of what happened, the eldest looking gentleman shook his head side to side resolutely and made a motion with his pipe drawing it across his chest in front of him. The couple nodded and pulled a rope from behind the drums. Hank grew concerned.

Hank was desperate to prove his good intentions. He forced his way to his feet and feigned the dance he'd witnessed from the top of the hill. The braves grabbed his arms and were about to force him down again when an old woman, perhaps a medicine woman, raised her pipe and spoke something in their language that caused the braves to stop. She waved her pipe.

She was beckoning Hank over. Slowly, and with intentional respect, he walked toward her. In front of her, wishing to show sincerity, he took his cowboy boots off. She smiled and handed him a leather vest. He stripped from the waist up, put on the vest and stood by the fire readying himself as best he could for whatever would come next. His woodworking build seemed to impress those assembled there.

At a signal from the woman the drums began again. With an open hand she directed Hank to join in the dance. It was as though she could intuit his intention though no words passed between them. Hank followed those around him and after several minutes had picked up the basics of the dance. Though some looked on in skepticism, cheers came from the crowd. He only imagined that the revelry kept everyone on the Western History Hotel awake that night. After several hours he was allowed to bow to the older woman, then paying respects to the elder man, returned the leather vest, put his boots back on, and returned to the hotel being sure to walk around the puddle of water.

He slept soundly but woke with the sunrise. The smell of bacon and other breakfast foods called him out of his room. At breakfast, he began to apologize for being part of the ruckus the evening before when Jeffry stopped him short.

"What ruckus?"

"Well, the drumming and dancing over yonder behind that hill to the west."

"Drumming did you say?"

"Yes, with the Native Americans."

"Oh, now I get it. Yes, they used to do that throughout the 1800s. It was especially prominent around the time of Custer. Whenever they had won a battle, they'd whoop up a storm, so the stories go.

"It was a celebration of victory to dance in circles while wearing vests of leather. The victories against the settlers were few, so they were celebrated heartily. You had me goin' there young man. You must have made use of the historical accounts in your room to come up with that one. You're in 1876, right? Heh, heh, you do like history. I could smell it on ya when you arrived."

"Yeah, that's right. I guess I was so sleepy that I dreamt it was real. I was pretty tired from all that drivin'."

"Real, huh? We hear that a lot here at the Western History Hotel. The dreams people have must be compelling as all get out." Hank was glad that he hadn't chosen the room Wounded Knee. On the porch Hank ran into another guest who was leaving.

"Hank did you say was your name? I'm Jed."

"Yup. Hank it is. Glad to meet you Jed."

"You didn't see any Homesteaders last night, did ya?"

"Afraid I didn't. Seems like each room has its own dreams that come with it."

"You can say that again. I never want to ride in a covered wagon again. That is a bumpy, hard ride. Not much of a dream at all."

"I can only imagine."

"I only have one regret from staying here last night," Hank said pensively.

"Yah, what's that?"

"Well we can't likely tell others of this. We'd never be believed."

"I don't care." It was the most fascinating night of my life."

"I must agree. The same is true for me."

"So long, Hank," Jed said as he moved toward his pickup truck.

"So long Jed," Hank said as he unlocked and opened his car to the smell of finished wood products. Hank felt awfully lucky. Unlike Custer and his men, he had returned alive.

Concert Pianist

His fingers march across the keyboard
to Elliot Carter's Piano Sonata
like soldiers in a 1945 victory parade;
then they tiptoed through Scarlotti's
D minor sonata and skipped
across the keys in D major,
passion flinging out
like ribbons from a May pole
leaving one weary, breathless.

When Mozart came to call,
his fingers pirouetted
on ebony and ivory
whirling, leap frogging
hand over hand,
pressing melody,
like cider, from black confetti sprinkled
furiously across the "face" spaces
and "every good boy deserves fudge" lines.

His slight of hand awed eyes,
caressed ears with each touch
and we could see him melt into

the piano, black and white keys
twining up his arms like a man
eating vine until there was nothing
but the world opening up, devouring us,
pulling us nearer to it's pounding heart
making us all feel musical and free.

—A. Carol Scott

A Knife in the Rice Paddies

Fiction: Wen Lu

Yu Fei had a pain in her abdomen and the pain was getting worse. She panted. She stood by the duck pens supporting herself with a bamboo shoulder pole with her blue tunic, black pants and rubber boots covered with mud. Her full jet hair was covered with speckles of mud. From the two duck pens, there were hundred ducks quacking simultaneously. The smell of animal droppings under the burning summer sun was intensively repugnant. She was sweating uncontrollably not knowing if the sweat was from her labor to pen in the animals or from the intense pain.

A vast field of rice paddies was next to the duck pens. The crop was ready for harvest. It turned out to be a year of bumper harvest with the rice straws heavily laden with rice. A short distance away her husband, Ping Zhao, was wading through the paddies hauling a large bunch of rice straws across his robust shoulder. As he laid the straws by the thresher, he was alarmed by what he saw.

"You look very ill, my woman," he said.

Seeing his strong body and darkly tanned face, she cried out: "I feel like I've been stabbed in my stomach." So he carried her home through the mud.

Zhao was distraught. The family had little money to spare, let alone to pay for expensive hospital costs. With the rice harvesting in season and the year round animal farm needing his attention, he could hardly afford to take time off from the field. He realized his wife with her pretty delicate figure was getting thinner. Once the prettiest bride in the valley, she looked thin enough to be blown away with a gust of wind. With her severe pain, he had no choice but to take her to see a doctor.

Their two story cement house, a symbol of his success in the 1970s, was located near the entrance of a hilly village close to their pens and paddies. There was a small pond in front of the house where villagers washed their muddy feet, hoes, clothes, etc. Children often played on the narrow shore paved with terraced wide slates. Zhao pulled out a barrow and helped Fei get situated in a chair on one side of the barrow and balanced the other side with bricks. He then pushed the barrow to the town.

After two hours and paying fifty cents, they learned that they needed to go to a large hospital to get a diagnosis as the township doctor could not assess which organ was affected. Zhao was even more distraught to hear this. It would take a full day to get to the city and miss one day's worth of work points—more losses.

Early in the morning Zhao took Fei in the barrow to the county hospital. He brought all their savings with him. The trip took him one and half hours across the steaming land of paddies and hills. The waiting for an order number and seeing a doctor took them another two hours. The doctor told him that she needed to be hospitalized right away. Zhao paid a deposit so that she was settled in the hospital and administered antibiotics immediately. However, after some diagnostic tests, the doctors became concerned of a serious illness and suggested she go to a more advanced hospital in a large city called Hangzhou.

The news was devastating to Zhao. The week-long hospital stay already depleted their savings. He had no choice but to reluctantly borrow from his and her families and friends. Running between the hospital and home, he neglected to sell the duck eggs which were piling up and soon spoiled, generating no farm income.

To Fei the news was like being stabbed in her stomach a second time. Not knowing what her illness was, nor how long and how much the medical treatment was going to be made her think of her own death. But her youth and optimism helped her to avoid those thoughts.

The couple asked their siblings and other relatives for small loans. Her parents volunteered all they had. In the end, they had one hundred yuan in hand. With that, Zhao took her to the best hospital in Zhejiang province.

When the diagnosis was complete, Zhao was called in to the doctor's office and in a round-about way, the doctor told him that his wife had late stage ovarian cancer. He was shell-shocked and exclaimed: "Cancer! She is dying? That cannot be, Doctor!" He collapsed to the chair. Then he begged: "Please save her, Doctor." The doctor consoled him with words that an experimental anticancer drug would be administered to her immediately at no cost to the patient. He just nodded with approval.

Neither Zhao nor the doctor told Fei about the diagnosis. Instead they told her that she had a chronic ulcer that needed several weeks of rest to recover. She was given the experimental medicine and pain killer intravenously every day. Totally broken and without any clue of what to do, Zhao went back to the village. With a grave heart, he delivered the news to both his and her families. Shock swept through the villages in the valley. Tears – many tears – were shed. Following custom, everyone agreed that Fei was not to be told about the diagnosis to spare her such bad news and allow her a peaceful departure from the world.

A week later Zhao returned to the hospital. Happy to see him, Fei complained about the uncomfortable surroundings and high costs of the hospital. Since the pain was gone, she wanted to go home. With "tears" in his heart, he said he would do as she requested. The doctor permitted her discharge from the hospital and instructed her to take the "antibiotics" four times a day. The antibiotics were actually morphine without her knowledge.

Fei was happy to be home. On her land she labored in the paddies and tended to the ducks; she cared for the crops, and cooked meals for the family. Though she felt weaker than before, she kept on going. Other villagers seldom talked to her nowadays. One night there was a wolf in the pen snatching ducks by the neck. Dozens of ducks were lost. On another day eggs were stolen. As a result, Zhao started to sleep in a tent next to the pens. Fei took care of their five year old son.

Soon autumn rice was planted. On a routine visit, she noticed one of her paddies was drained and under the scorching summer sun, the soil was left to dry and the rice shoots were nearly baked. The paddies downstream were brimmed with water. "Who is sabotaging my land?" She was furious. "Curse you, lynched corpse. Curse you, headless ghost." She yelled out loud and started a quarrel with a villager in the downstream paddies. At one point Fei slapped his face with all her strength.

The man charged back, pushed her backwards, and shouted: "You, a dying woman! Save that energy for hell. Every villager knows that you have terminal cancer!"

Fei collapsed. For a minute she looked lifeless. She tried to hold herself upright, but did not have the strength. She wanted to yell, but did not have the voice. She fell into the mud in the paddy. Her mind went blank and her spirit momentarily left her. The villagers carried her home. From then on no one ever saw her stand up again. Some people said she broke her spine when she fell in the paddies. Other people said there was a knife in the paddies that spear-cut her spine. Day in and day out, she lay in bed completely supported by her husband who cooked for her, fed her, carried her to potty, cleaned her, and burned incense for her.

It was autumn. Cassia trees emitted their last fragrance in the valley and leaves swirled with the wind on the last warm days before the winter. Fei suffered the worst pain. The pain was becoming unbearable. Every day, Zhao took her to a nearby hospital to get shots of the strongest pain reliever available. Family members knew that her last days were near and came to see her bringing food, gifts, and money.

Just as everybody thought she was drifting away from her people and the world around her, a miracle happened. One day she woke up from her usual drowsiness and was well enough to sit up. Her son, seeing his mother in good spirit, climbed up on her bed and asked mama to play with him. Fei pleasantly cooperated. They played joker. Then the boy heard children's voices outside and said he was going to play with his little neighbors near the pond.

Out he dashed and Fei was suddenly agitated and called out: "Son, my treasure! Watch out." She struggled to get off her bed and moved to the front door with the support of furniture. She saw a neighbor's two year old child in the water. Without any hesitation she tried to run towards the child, but fell to the ground. She then crawled to the pond stretching her hand out to the child in the water. The child reached for her hand and was saved, but she slid under the water.

The family buried Fei on a hill facing the village. Zhao wept in front of the black and white wedding photo of he and Fei and murmured incoherently: "My fault... sorry...so many regrets..." He lit an incense stick, held it with two hands, and bowed to her thrice, as did his son.

Otto

The man was a '78 Chevy,
white four-door sedan.
Once a red Corvette living shiny,
The black leather interior
was a virtual paint brush
from which no town was safe.

His tour started on wheels –
three – progressed on two
graduated on four – a Ford,
basic, pale gray, blue inside,
blasé, Iowa farm boy blasé.

When he discovered spark plugs
his journey sped forward;
cruising on premium
lubricating with the best.

Now, the white '78 Chevy
gives no hint of the Corvette;
spark plugs fire unevenly
jumper cables in the trunk

but hidden in the glove box,
dressed in a black leather pouch
the Corvette owner's manual
and a well-worn key . . .
residual history still humming
in the heart of a '78 Chevy.

—A. Carol Scott

Incident at Pipestone

Fiction: James Robert Kane

Sarah Strong Calf sat cross-legged and trembling on a broad ledge in her ancestral quarry near Pipestone, MN, infant daughter at her breast.

Her destiny, so clearly defined through a series of visions, hung in the early morning darkness before her, like ripe grain waiting for harvest. Yet she could not claim it. The spirits who sent the visions had suddenly demanded one more sacrifice, and the price could not have been higher.

The infant finished suckling and Sarah set her tenderly into her lap. Just to her right lay a nine-inch shard of quartzite, and her fingers trembled as they explored its razor sharp edge. The baby gurgled and cooed and smiled in satisfied comfort as Sarah barely breathed, steeling herself.

It was not supposed to be this way.

Three days ago the Spirits of the Four Directions sang their mesmerizing song, validating her destiny vision and propelling Sarah, Billy Youngblood and their daughter to this holy place. Everything was finally in alignment.

They had been been anticipating this moment for what seemed like an eternity, ever since Sarah emerged from a prolonged vision trance convinced that Billy would become a pipe carrier and she a powerful medicine woman. Neither had reason to doubt. The granddaughter of a medicine woman, her formidable access to the spirit world was already widely acclaimed. She seemed a conduit for special ancestral knowledge. Billy's blood flowed from a long line of pipe carriers, who used its mystical powers to serve their people. Tribal elders had experienced positive dreams about his abilities and dedication. Sarah fully expected that they would become a powerful force for everything good.

There was just one problem. Billy had no pipe. Traditionally a father might pass his sacred pipe down to his son, but Billy's father's pipe went to the grave with him. He needed to craft his own, and so Billy needed to dig.

Sarah and Billy understood why every generation before them had nearly broken their backs trying to shatter the thick deposit of hard, reddish-pink quartzite and expose the treasured, elusive strata of pipestone; believed that it was formed from the blood of the ancient ones, all that was left of their people after the great flood; that they were made from it, and that even the ground containing it was sacred.

And so they prayed, fasted, made offerings and painted their bodies before attacking seams in the stubborn rock. Billy set his hips and shoulders into every arc of his sledgehammer, driving his wedges ever deeper, expanding each seam incrementally towards fracture. But the broken rock yielded only disappointment as Sarah lugged it to the slag heap at the rim, and exhaustion stopped them well before sunset.

Sarah knew only one thing could bring them success, so

that night, as Billy slept completely spent, Sarah crawled from their small tent and, armed with the Sacred Medicine Bundle inherited from her grandmother, returned with her baby to the ledge

There, atop a blanket woven by that woman and blessed in her pipe carrier's smoke, Sarah began a quiet chanting as she carefully unpacked the bundle. It contained many small objects (seeds, crystals, arrowheads, and more) tied up in scraps of buckskin or gut casings, some handed down through so many generations that their imprecise origins had become the stuff of mythology. Each one, sacred to its originator. Sarah had added three: a lock of Billy's hair, tobacco grown by her father and a birth poem from her mother. Each she reverently held skyward before repacking and pressing the bundle to her heart, waiting for uplifting direction. Instead, the unthinkable.

She replayed the events in her mind again, just to be sure she had done everything correctly, re-examining every vision and dream, listening again to the spirit song, feeling anew the power of the Sacred Medicine Bundle. And in her heart she knew she had been true.

The baby wriggled as it played with the waist-length, black braid spilling over Sarah's shoulder and the movement jolted her back to real time. Back to that ledge and her destiny. She couldn't put it off any longer. The spirits were waiting.

Sarah swallowed hard, crying as she peeled off her shirt and wrapped one end of the lethal tool. Heart pounding, she forced the blade high, paused to offer one more plea for mercy, and, when no answer came, obeyed.

She did not feel time pause, warp and envelop her; did not feel the spirits redirect her hand nor the silky smooth side of the shard slide along the back of her neck just as the moment ended. She only felt the braid slide off her shoulder and fall lifeless onto her delighted baby.

Stunned, she sat motionless as the impact of what happened hit her, then scooped up the child and smothered it with kisses. She had passed the test. Had been allowed to trade one sacrifice for another. The baby for the braid. Her precious child for what she had always believed was the source of her power. She could only hope she was still whole.

Drained, she wrapped herself and the baby in the blanket, and, with the sacred bundle for a pillow, let sleep claim her.

Come sunrise began the beckoning.

It came sounding at first like grasses whispering tenderly in dawn's respiration, but as Sarah listened more closely knew it was something else. Clutching her daughter she abandoned the blanket for the crisp morning air and, following the sound, crept along the ledge and down, to a layer long abandoned as unproductive. There, flowing gently from a seam, she felt the breath of her ancestors against her face.

"Here," the breath said to her. "Here."

Dear Pug

Last time I saw you
I heard you singin'
'I Love You Truly'
at my weddin'
you'uz drivin'
a beat up old '50 Chevy,
grey, I think, had
a blue trunk door
after you backed into
that semi of squeelin' pigs
bound for the yards.
I can still hear your Paw
yellin'; he's gone now I heard.
After the ceremony we cruised
through town in Milt's red
59 Pontiac convertible,
top down a course,
horns honkin',
all of us laughin' and wavin'.
Lost touch after that.
you headed off to the Far East
and Sweet and me, well we just
headed off into life
all eager and confident.
Had that cute little red bug

remember, was all we could afford.
Sweet and me paid just over $1700 for it
it was pretty small
kind of like the world
we were lauchin' into back then,
but it was new;
only had 8 blasted miles on it.
I'd give bout anything
to have that bug back now.
Then Sweet started singin'.
Got so good birds fell
from the sky ashamed of
their own dissonance.
But we'uz doin' pretty good by then.
Got us a big Chrysler.
Real up-town you know—
Was a dark navy blue
With a fancy dash board
so full of glowin' dials
it looked like a cock pit.
Ohh, we looked real good in that car.
Well, that was long ago.

I know Nam wasn't too good to you
but I heard you did ok.
Milt said after the war you got yourself
one of those VW vans with flowers
painted on the side, like a hippie.

'Zat true?
Next I know you'd opened a leather shop
somewheres in the Midwest,
Illinois was it?
Done pretty good too I heard.
Is it true you got yourself a snow white caddy?

Sweet's gone now,
whisked off too soon.
I can still see her flower
draped copper box
riding so proud
in that shiny black hearse.
I'm retired now. Surrounded
by cemetery silence.
Sweet's marble stone's
sittin' right where my heart once beat.

My vehicle of choice these days
has two wheels—
lost my legs to sugar
a few years back.
Don't go too much any more
the old engine's running low

on fuel. Come see me in that
new Intrepid a yours.
Sweet memories, Stan.

—A. Carol Scott

Mozart Age Five

A peculiar child
gossamer in frame
every hair on his arm
points— pricked as a pin

He sits
a fledgling
craving every drop
each pitch of the harpsichord creeps
along his petticoat, his knickers,
his stockings.

—Susana Hanson

Alone in the North Carolina Woods –1840

Fiction: Mona Gustafson Affinito

A mama can't lose her child and still stay strong - not this mama anyway. Horace had to insist on going after the bear that bloodied our baby to death. It didn't matter that I begged him not to. I need him here, not off crackling through the woods, tracking that crazed killer. I need him to fetch water from the creek, to lift the kettle over the fire. I need him to see all my strength has poured out of me.

The snapping of underbrush outside slices through me like an arrow, tearing invisible shreds from my insides. Maybe it wasn't a Cherokee I heard. Maybe it was the bear, or the bear's baby. Or, good Lord forbid, maybe it's Horace limping home to die. I could be left alone in this God-abandoned place.

Something is crunching the autumn underbrush outside. The heavy, rhythmic steps of an animal determined to do me harm? I can't leave the kitchen fire. The flames could spread. Leaving us with nothing. I can't stay here.

I can't leave.

I hate this place. I hate this pile of logs called a house. I hate the pitch holding them together. I hate the smell of pine and laurel. I hate being so far away from people. I hate being alone in my grief. I hate the darkness. I hate that Horace went off on his fool's errand. My hands clutch frantically at my petticoats, finding no relief in the action.

The footsteps are coming nearer, loud like the giant in a child's fairy tale. My second baby pounces on my insides.

I can't stay in the kitchen. I douse the fire and head across the dog's way to the bedroom, not that I'm any safer there, but somehow it just feels better.

Horace took his rifle and left the Winchester for me. I've practiced using it on small game and such, but my hands twitch at the thought of looking an Indian or a bear in the eye, to say nothing of shooting. Truth be told, my hands are trembling too much to hold anything right now.

I cling to the bedpost, caressing the finialed reminder of more civilized days. It came with us from Virginia. It warms me with its lingering heavy, briny scent of Williamsburg, evoking the beauty of the boxwoods. More sad than comforting, it betokens love and family and home. My second little one is calming down a bit inside me.

Footsteps in the dog's way!

"Horace? Horace? Is that you?"

No answer.

At first nothing comes out when I try to open my throat. Then, choked and weak, "Horace, help!"

A vaguely familiar but strange man steps hesitantly, almost apologetically, into the bedroom, carrying a small box--a coffin for our mauled child.

Tears in his eyes, he gestures toward his throat and then to the gift he offers. He crosses himself and holds the box out to me. The little coffin opens a gush of salt mixed with some kind of human river and my tears flow down unchecked to soak my apron as my legs collapse under me.

The stranger catches me and guides me to rest, leaning on the edge of the bed. Then he hands me a note written with the sweet touch of a female hand.

Please accept this gift for your dear child. My husband has been unable to speak ever since an arrow passed through his throat five years ago. But word of your grief traveled many miles across the creek to reach us in the town of Marburg. Please let us be your aid and support.

Horace comes running in, rifle at the ready. I rush from the bed to block his entrance in fear that he will destroy our benefactor. He lowers his gun. I embrace him. I hate him. I love him. I love the kindness of neighbors. I hate this place. Where is my place?

I want to go home.

Just in Time to Say Goodbye

Creative nonfiction: Mona Gustafson Affinito

I made it in time, half way across the country.

"Mom's waiting for you." Eddie gestured toward my lifelong friend, seemingly comatose on the Hospice bed. I held her hand. I think she squeezed mine a little.

"She had some prune juice for breakfast this morning," he said. "And she asked when you would be coming."

My last chance to talk with the person who held so much of my life in her hands, from the time we were in our carriages, I think. Certainly from tricycle days.

"Remember riding down our hill tilting your tricycle to make it a two-wheeler? With me following cautiously behind on three wheels?" I asked. Her eyes fluttered slightly open, then closed. Hallie was always good at eye-fluttering.

I think a little smile played on her lips as I went on. "Playing marbles for keepsies? The only game I was good at. You even picked more violets for Mother's Day. Boyfriends at BayView beach? Spotting for enemy planes during the war? I couldn't tell a plane from a mosquito. Giggling at your wedding; crying at my college graduation? Oh, and always protecting me from the scary neighborhood dogs?"

Hallie laughed, full-bellied as she used to, and drifted away to the end of her journey.

After the Fact

A room with too much air between
the cracks. Too much shrink
like a limp balloon sucking breath.
And he asks: "What do you want
for breakfast?"

And then
the falling
recalling the starfish
on his boxers—
the sweat and his neck
print of his thumb
wearing my cheek...

Cheerios and juice
I swallow his
bowl of lies
and his eyes
grey
inside me
like steal
daggers
stuffed

with arrogance
too much arrogance to hide
the offense

too much to gloss over it
the error
the inconsistent pulse
of his breath...

—Susana Hanson

These Things I Put In A Box
Excerpt

I. The Knowing

I cannot comprehend
the granite-crack inside
my chest, The Feeling, too big
for my skin, my veins
like amber turning inside out
scrape the chambers where my organs sleep
crawl the corners of the vessel

In this
I exist

I breathe
I hurt   deep

in the place
where the creases
of my pores
soak it in
   soak the words
the sting, and the ache
assault my eyes-ducts
and what remains
is   still

II. The Father

He stood there
staring her every inch
incubated
like one more   second
might make
   the difference
might i m p r i n t   her
face
in the folds of his brain

V. The Box.

There is a box of you
I carry it with me

sometimes in my pocket
a shred of my heart

and sometimes it fills
the entire room
stealing my air supply
can't catch my breath
sometime I can feel it
on my eyelashes
or the bottom
of my toes, the pores on my face,
the tip of my toenail

sometimes it clings to the edge
of my t-shirt when I do the laundry
I can feel it when my feet scape the tile

it follows me
this box of you

—Susana Hanson

As I Love You Now:
A Letter To Him

I sit here in a coffee shop, and you, might be sitting two seats
over, or maybe,
somewhere in Boston, or Greece, or Cambodia, or maybe, you
spend time wandering
wandering the hills of the North Shore; tiptoeing along the
pebbles
where my toes danced hot, hot on smooth stone. Searching for
me.

But for now, you carry me with you, as I carry you,
the way swans carry their young, nestled bunch, heap of feathers.
And you are everywhere and always speak my name. You
understand my every curve
each inch. You have known me forever, like moss knows rock,
like salt knows sea, like silt knows quartz, like veins know blood.
Like I

know you. You are instilled in me, like a ticking clock inside a
tower,
or the button that clings to my breast-coat pocket, or the freckle
on my cheek and the scar on my wrist, from the boy
who stabbed me with a pencil in the eighth grade.

And we continue this knowing until the day we meet. Maybe we have met before and I have already loved you as I love you now, as I love you this moment.

—Susana Hanson

The Quaint Angel

Her face was haloed by a bright sun
that hung above Heavens gate.

She had the countenance of a Botticelli angel.
Her porcelain skin was smooth like alabaster.

God had spared her the encumbrance of wings,
in favor of long fingers and a thin neck.

She is called "The Quiet One",
for she chooses to speak in whispers.

She is the white child,
the child of large brown eyes and the quaint smile.

> The child is fair,
> her feet are soft and light.
>
> You would believe
> she walks on air.
>
> You would believe
> she's been given flight.

—B.D. Smith

Contacts

Fiction: Anne Jackson

Contacts. Open, scroll, scroll, "Jonathan," delete.

Old mommy friend, no wait, acquaintance from dance class 2 years ago...delete.

"Lisa"—BITCH—DELETE Can I hard delete a person?

Scroll, keep, keep, keep.

I glance at my watch. Half an hour before the swim meet ends, and Lucy's last event isn't until the end. I look around. She is hunkered down with pals munching snacks and doing homework. I guiltlessly settle back into my rare moment of alone time, doing something for myself, like cleaning out my contacts list.

Scroll, What? "The LORD." I look around and back at my phone. There is a number here I don't recognize. Has one of my wittier co-workers spent quality time with my phone lately? I consider it but don't think so. Hmmm. Weird.

Delete?...No...

Scroll down, scroll down. Cast a glance around...scroll back scroll back.

Touch contact "The LORD."

Text contact.

"Are you there God? It's me Margaret."

I hit send and pause, anticipating a snappy comeback from the friend who did this.

Ping "I am, and you are not."

Text "I'm not what?"

Ping "Margaret. I know all about you, Beverly."

Text "You are creeping me out."

Ping "Fear not."

Text "ha ha"

Nothing.

Text "What is my favorite color?"

Ping "Orange."

Text "What is my favorite peanut butter sandwich?"

Ping "Wheat toast, peanut butter and dill pickle coins, not slices."

Text "What color are the underwear I am wearing right now?"

Ping "You need to do laundry so you are wearing the white full brief style you bought after you had Lucy that you keep in the back of the drawer and wear for comfort when your husband is out of town."

I set the phone down like a stick of dynamite on the chlorine spotted plastic table next to my purse. I look around the room suspiciously, waiting for a camera crew to bust out of the girls' shower room. Everything looks normal. I look back at my phone, half expecting it to be looking back at me. I pick the phone back up, take a deep breath and let it out slowly ala the yoga I used to do.

Text "You can't be who you say you are, but how else would you know all those things?"

Nothing.

Text "How do I know it is You?"

Ping "Faith."

Text "What if I don't believe?"

Ping "Try harder."

Text "If You are You, why do bad things happen? Why are good people murdered? Why do children starve?"

Ping "Free will."

Text "Cop out. We are Your creation. Make us perfect."

Ping "You had your chance."

Text "Touché."

I look around and check to see if the world around me has gone mad. Everything is still normal. I focus back on my phone, shaken, wondering what to ask next. I consider asking why is the door handle on the fifth floor access to the elevators always warm, why do men look better as they age and women look used up, why my father got sick.

Ping "I Love You."

Text "I love you."

Ping "You should love yourself better. You are My wonderful creation."

Text "I love my child. I love my husband. I love myself."

Ping "Not like you should."

Text "How should I love?"

Ping "Through My eyes."

Text "I don't know if I can."

Ping "Try harder."

Text "How?"

Ping "Through Me."

Text "Oh. How do I do that?"

Ping "Surrender."

Text "Try harder by quitting? I don't understand."

Ping "Not quit. Surrender. Trust that I will handle things for you, through you."

Text "Oh, I don't let go well."

Ping "I know."

Text "Yeah."

I sigh deeply. Is this real or am I a fool? Does it matter? I see Lucy packing up her homework and preparing to warm up for her race. Almost time to be Mom again. I look at my phone.

I text, "Am I enough?" and hit send before I can chicken out.

Ping "No."

My heart pinches in my chest.

Ping "But I am."

I stare.

"Mom." Lucy's voice startles me. I look up and she gestures at the clock. Her race starts soon and I should go over to watch. I look back at my phone stupidly, hesitating. "Mom!" Lucy's yell insists. I snag my purse and chuck my phone into it as I walk towards her.

"Blurp." I take a few more steps before the sound registers. This is the sound my phone made as it slid past my open purse and fell into the pool.

I pause and look back at the nice swim capped girl who has stopped her practice lap to hand me my surely dead phone with a rueful smile.

"Oh." This is the tiny sound I make as I register that what just happened can never be shared or proven to anyone.

I take the phone and hold it like the dead fish it is between two fingers as I walk to see the last race of the day.

Interrupted Honeymoon

Fiction: Heidi Skarie

Toemeka Kimes disembarked from the Viper 4X, a two-person spacecraft, and paused. She felt an uneasy feeling in the pit of her stomach. She turned to Michio, still amazed that this deeply spiritual, handsome man was her husband. They'd only been married two days.

"It isn't safe for us to be on Ryhu," she said. "I sense danger."

He frowned. "It's a neutral planet. I've never run into trouble here."

"Perhaps things have changed."

"It's possible. We should be on guard. I need to order supplies for the domed city of Kanai. The outpost colony isn't established enough to be self-sustaining."

"I thought we came here for a honeymoon." Disappointment flooded through her.

"We did." He looked at her with eyes full of love. "I booked us a beautiful overwater bungalow. We'll go there as soon as my business is complete."

"What a wonderful surprise!" Toemeka kissed him, accepting the unexpected side trip. The galaxy was at war and she was accustomed to risk as an undercover operative for the Coalition of Independent Nations.

A few hours later, Toemeka and Michio entered a small store and approached the green-skinned humanoid who stood behind the sales counter. "Greetings, Yender. It's good to see you, again," Michio said.

"Michio, it's been awhile." The gills on the sides of Yender's head opened and closed—a clear sign that he was nervous. "Who is this exotic creature with you?"

Toemeka sensed he was really asking if she could be trusted.

"My wife, Toemeka."

"You took a mate. Is that wise in your line of work?" He pulled out a communicator and showed them a "Wanted Dead or Alive" picture of Michio. "Samrat Condor increased the bounty on your head. He's not happy that you killed General Bhandar and freed the country of Jaipar. Pictures of you are being broadcasted all over Ryhu's Internet. Just yesterday a bounty hunter was here asking about you."

Michio's expression remained serene. "I need supplies."

"I can't help you. It's gotten too dangerous."

"I'll pay you double. Half now and half upon delivery. Drop the supplies off at the Endma space station and I'll make arrangements to pick them up there."

Toemeka watched the man's round gold eyes as he

wrestled with fear versus greed. *I don't trust him,* she said telepathically to Michio.

He can be counted on to deliver supplies, but beyond that I don't trust him either, he replied inwardly. *We'll disappear after this transaction.*

Finally Yender said, "All right, I'll do it, but this is the last time."

While he and Michio discussed the order details, Toemeka uneasily scanned the shop. There weren't any other customers at the moment.

* * *

Deep in the ocean, joy filled Toemeka when she spotted a school of tarami fish and she enthusiastically pointed them out to Michio. After ordering supplies they'd checked into their bungalow and decided to go diving. She'd been pleased to discover Michio was also an experienced diver. There was still much to learn about him. They'd only known each other a few months and during most of that time they'd been involved in an undercover operation that had left little personal time.

When the mission was over, she received orders to return to Coalition headquarters to defend Alandra from an impending attack by Samrat Condor's air fleet. Instead, she stayed with Michio, but part of her still wanted to be with her team—defending Alandra. She still didn't know if she'd made the right decision.

Swimming among the fish and other sea creatures, she felt as if she was in a different world. A bright blue, star dolphin swam by and she followed it, circling around a large rock formation. After awhile she glanced over her shoulder, expecting to find Michio there. When she didn't see him, she started swimming back, knowing they needed to stay close. Finally she spotted him and gasped. He was fighting another diver! The attacker cut Michio's hoses, then shot away on a motorized device.

No! Michio can't die! she thought as she frantically swam toward her husband, cursing herself for not staying near him. When she reached him, he grabbed the buddy regulator attached to her air tank and put it in his mouth. She held onto his arm to keep them together as he took a couple of breaths

Thank God you realized I wasn't with you and came back! he said telepathically. *That diver took me completely by surprise.*

Are you all right?

I am now. He looked at her with concern. *You're breathing too fast. Try to calm down or you'll use up the air supply too quickly.*

Give me a minute. By the stars, Michio, you almost drowned.

We're going to make it, sweetheart. We need to ascend slowly in stages.

I know. I'm just nervous being this far under water with

that bounty hunter lurking around. She focused inwardly and moved into a contemplative state. Gradually her breathing slowed and they began their ascent, holding hands and going up in intervals.

At last they broke surface and swam to shore. Once on land, Michio held Toemeka in his arms. "Is your intuition always so accurate?"

"Not always." She could tell by the tension in Michio's body he was also shaken.

"Thank you for saving my life. We'd better leave this planet."

At the spaceport, Michio and Toemeka carried their travel bags across the airfield. They almost reached the Viper when Michio pulled her behind a spaceship.

"The bounty hunter's waiting for us!" Michio said. "He's by the traffic control tower."

"How will we get to the Viper?"

"I think this is a good time to teach you the art of invisibility."

She raised her eyebrows dubiously. How could she learn such a difficult skill in such a short time? "Wouldn't it be easier if I just walked over to the ship and taxied it over to you?"

"Too risky. He might shoot you. To disguise our presence from the bounty hunter we'll have to ascertain his rate of vibration, then raise our own vibrations to an exact tone above his so he won't detect our presence."

"How will we do that?"

"Intuitively sense his aura, then hear the harmonic tone above it and shift to that level."

"Are you sure this will work?"

"The method isn't flawless, but the bounty hunter has a fairly low state of awareness, so it will be easy to rise above it. The hardest part is the amount of focus it takes to stay on a high harmonic level. But don't be concerned. I'll help you."

Toemeka focused on the bounty hunter and soon felt his energy. Then Michio said inwardly, *You're a child of God.* His words lifted her vibrations to an ideal harmony above the assassin's. Michio's emerald eyes met hers and he nodded. They hurried across the tarmac, staying in the shadows and behind ships. As they drew closer to the bounty hunter, Toemeka felt her concentration slipping and started running. Michio hit the ship's keyless remote—its canopy opened and the engines started.

They jumped into the cockpit and put up the energy shields. A missile exploded against the side of the ship, rocking them violently. "Get us out of here, Michio!" Toemeka yelled. A second later the ship soared upward.

Once they were out of danger, Toemeka slumped back in her chair, feeling drained. "What a terrible honeymoon," she said. "I almost became a widow."

He reached out and lovingly squeezed her hand. "We'll plan another one that doesn't involve a dangerous business transaction."

"I'm content with the gift of a live husband. When I married you and took a leave of absence from the Coalition, I thought I was deserting the fight against Samrat Condor. Now it appears I'm still involved in the war in an even more important way."

"I'm afraid so. You stepped closer to the center of the fight. I wish it wasn't true. I was looking forward to our honeymoon."

"So was I, but I'd rather be at your side than any other place in the galaxy, even if it is dangerous."

Book Break

Sunshine nudged my arm,
coaxed me from my story
just in time to spy
red angus wearing
silver earrings graze near
monstrous marshmallows,

toasted hay bales,
products of a so close shave
on blade-scraped fields.

Beside the highway
beardless prairie mirrored
sheared remnant table ends;
plush corduroy and
nubby caramel wool
brushed honey/emerald plaid;

choices that would wear well
on those who know
their business, singing,

"Bringing in the sheaves,"
on Sunday morning at

a fine country church
built of Norway pine,
sturdy stuff for standing
weather, whatever;

even lutefisk suppers
serving "all the lefse
you can eat."

Suddenly the sun
went in and chilled without,
I blinked and shivered,
wrapped a tawny shawl
around my cold shoulders,
let my gaze fall,

my spanned attention
crawl into the pages
of my still warm book.

—Bethany Hammer

Travel Things Observed

Leather Suitcase: Dead Weight

Carry-on
Carrion.

Universal Design

God
Universe
Galaxy
World
Hemisphere
Continent
Country
Mountain range
State
Panorama
Foothill
Forest
Grove
Tree
Branch
Tuft
Needle
Xylem
Cell
Mitochondria
Nucleus
God.   —Angela Hunt

Erik the Red Meat Shopper

At the Scandinavian market
Only the rich can buy food
But that's ok, they are all rich.
One would think I am too, for I am here,
¾ impostor in my version of corn silk hair
And sage eyes.

Butchers' scales weigh status;
Pies chart each man's capacity.
Varieties of sweets reveal
The acquired tastes of world travel;
Fresh produce registers lumens of hunger for sunlight.
A society, shelved in microcosm:

Organic hydroponic ingenuity
(agri-business challenging winter's solstice)
Congeniality
(a prawn monger constitutionally
 confident of his next meal)
Quality of life
(customer assurance fresh will again be here next week)
Pragmatism
 (select only what is necessary)
And Norwegian sensibility
(cash purchases walked home in two fabric bags).

—Angela Hunt

A Quiet Earth (K'aua'i)

Breathy fog whispers to
Brainy convolutions of
Terra firma and verdant flora
In the wettest place on earth.

Fog flexes its fingers
Softens stiff ridges
Calms angry peaks
Soothes jagged edges
Mends torn places
Covers me with the palm of its hand.

We stare at each other
Face to face
The canyon and I
Both mute
In the mist of silence
Grateful
We do not demand words of each other.

—Angela Hunt

A Blazing Glimmering Lake
"Up North"

The day dawns still and crisp.
A skin of ice covers the water to the east,
A morning stubble of black saplings outlines the mouth of a stream
Where Beaver skinny dips in the frosty water, pattering mud
Over a lumpy lodge to keep his family snug in the coming months.

Tentative rays peek between land and low-hanging sky.
The boldest ones are grey,
Then by turns they all appear: violet, purple, puce
Mauve, cimarron, rose, shocking pink,
Orange, tangerine, peach,
Lavender, amber
And finally, Regent appears

At the end of the opulent procession;
Flashing a blindingly brilliant white-gold grin
Before tucking back under the steel velvet cloud cover
For a few more winks

And I realize
Beaver and I
Have plenty to be thankful for
Without Anyone
Saying a word.

Published in Chaska Herald 11/21/2012. Published in Minnesota PenWomen
e-Newsletter 2/2015. Posted on National PenWomen website as Poem of the Week
2/29/2015.

Untitled

White-hushed forest hope
Sequin-laden branches
Fashion-forward scarved

Slow Thaw

Springish stream of the slow pulse
Poised sculpted snow
Folding into black water.

Not Enough Spring

Entrepreneurial geese
Slushed arteries,
A brown waking place.

—Angela Hunt

Honored In Honduras

A trip to teach English
Slung 5 echelons away from Minnesota,
Each trajectory shorter than the one before;
The last leg, suitcases of books weighed
On a meat hook, vital statistics recorded
With pencil stub on tablet in case the jungle swallows.

3 got on a plane (sounding more like a joke than a journey):
a pilot, Ingles? Nada.
a missionary, nested among her suitcases
a young man, diamond dollar-sign necklace, his crucifix?
A single engine braved the happy Honduran sky over rainforest
canopy;
The little engine thought she could.
An uneventful liftoff, half an hour over lush interwoven
greens.
A thought: crashed wreckage could never be found. Then
A falter, a spray of oil on windshield.
Pilot using wipers again again...again only to see slow
descent. A cutting out.
The silence of moments, of breeze under wings, of chugged
and failed restarts.
A sloth-sequence of events:

Of spider monkeys shaking fists and screaming "Invasion!"
from emergent trees.
Of angry-eyeing macaws roused out of afternoon naps.
Of beauty surrounding and sunlight flashing scenes of lives lived.
Of polyglot agreement this would be a good time to pray.
Of complete calm. Of thinking this is a good day to die. Of
confident prayer.

Of assuredly telling Pilot, "Now try the engine one more time."
Of leaves curiously reaching toward a skimming plane belly.
Of engine, shy
Of oil, catching, starting, purring another 34 minutes to a
perfect landing.

Of villagers warmly surrounding the plane.
Dollar Sign telling the saga
Thanking God for honoring us with life.
Then grinning, considering
A chance to learn English
An even greater miracle.

—Angela Hunt

Aurora Borealis Dangling Above The Arctic Circle

Creative Nonfiction: Angela Hunt

June 6, 8:40 PM Flight over Southampton Island: a sentinel of a place. Frozen natural structures hang on for dear life to the sheer west face of rock. Wind and gravity and cold and sun contest each other over the huge objects. One iceberg cracks, "Gun schoel!" to the others, loses his grip, makes a heart-stopping plunge into the frigid water, holds his breath past passing out, then bobs to the surface, forcing a mammoth wave to echo "Sorry!" at the shore.

Northern Lights: bold baby blue above, pale-horse pink to butter below. A persuasion of smooth clouds overtakes the scape. As minutes drift by and the plane gallops north, an indigo band separates a lace sky from graying waves of silk below. Clouds are deep as a featherbed, calm as a bass lake at sunrise. A glint from window frost needle-pierces the quiet scene.

9:20 PM An echo-soft blue makes an open-faced sandwich on the horizon. Rivers of cloud undulate sensually, envelop the plane, parting long enough to get a glimpse of southern Baffin Island. Three broad rivers of earth and snow and ice appear to flow south, but the land is motionless. The sky broadens into a knowing grin.

9:35 PM The firmament becomes an ethereal phosphorescent white. Greenland's fjords sport blotchy snow, sparse shrubs and sudsy pumice. Curdled-milk icebergs impress upon the shore. Above, indecisive clouds.

10:10 PM The eyelids of the world are closing. Clouds are only crows' feet now. The horizon shows merely the difference between grey and gray. Forever is the only thing present.

12:00 Midnight Precisely half of a moon is dangling from a NW hook. The azure haze bank is christened with mauve. Above are stately waves pulsing toward a never-ending celestial shore. Above that, transparent, endless predawn. A jalopy-down-a-dusty-road jet stream is headed toward the pole, laughing all the way. Below us: now. Why has every other passenger shut blinds and eyes in sleep?

12:15 AM Behind, a moon, half-wide as a morning yawn, greeting our ever day. Already the sky has become ice blue. Endless dunes of snow below with low sun casting heavy shadows on ridges, washing every face. Completely present nothingness.

12:20 AM Now the white drip of a moon, an ornament dangling. Clouds: frothy, gyrating, regurgitating. The plane seeming not to move, stuck in the throat of the sky. Wave after wave of drifts and clouds, clouds and drifts, now jagged, honeycombed mountain peaks of dirty ice iced with snow, piled up shoulder to shoulder, standing room only. Ever north we move as the sun rises on grand ice clawing at the plane.

There is a sense of most humble omniscience to see the top third of the world-- yet we are only a couple thousand feet above Greenland. What a fearsome, lonely, awesome, barren, beautiful, austere land this is: the convoluted gray matter of the world.

12:30 AM Banty-henned feathers of snow, the ribs of omni-directional drifts. Where is my Inuktitut vocabulary? 54 words for snow lost in the wonder of it all, the tiny 747 the only human-made shadow anywhere. Now fissures, crazing the glaze of this porcelain saucer Earth. Pattern. Repetition. Symmetry. Tessellation. Mammary moguls, breasts of ice, enough to water the world.

12:45 AM Night has been pronounced "Over". Sunrise is finished. A plateau has exalted itself above the landscape. The moon has become an apostrophe, reminding me the only One who can use the possessive case here is God Himself. Mackerel sky echoes mackerel earth, blue ocean slush forming a river through water-laden snow and honeycomb ice as we enter the Denmark Strait, 40 minutes from Iceland.

1:15AM has become 6:15 AM. Iceland is surreal: green ice hot springs, oases among south facing sand dunes. A milk-chocolate dinner plate of a lake dead ahead as we turn east. Powder blue of sky and ice, and clear white of cloud and land are married as Wedgwood, with an aluminum ocean below. Claws of rock with webs of snow between the toes have given way to cranial plates of glacier fit together in one great converging skull, parietal forgiving, and occipital being forgiven. Ice water runs in veins. We prepare for landing with two layers of cirrus clouds laminating over drifts of volcanic soil. A wash of litmus haze tests the bright white horizon. The greeting: a horde of purple lupines. A plover flushes out as we land. Iceland is also fertile moonscape with green grass and hazelnut shrubbery. It is agrarian with Old Faithful vents, orange and jade streams of mineral glacial runoff, and mud baths. There are miles of emerald fields lined with orange beaches against cobalt shores finished with a crust of icebergs. It is a Caribbean spa on ice.

About Our Authors

Mona Gustafson Affinito Ph.D, L.P. is Emeritus Professor of Psychology at Southern Connecticut State University and The Alfred Adler Graduate School. In private practice for over forty years, she currently sees clients in Chaska, Minnesota. Mona is the author of several books: "When to Forgive," "Forgiving One Page at a Time," "Mrs. Job," and "Figs & Pomegranates & Special Cheeses."

Kristin M. Arneson is an artist and art educator, a pianist and poet. She is a professor emerita with a Bachelor's degree and Master's degree in art from Dominican University. Her haiku poems were composed while walking and meditating on the trail between Chaska and Carver and were then published with a copyright in the Edge Magazine.

S.C. Bresson (Sherrie Anderson) is a native Minnesotan. She has a lively imagination and loves to write. She reads voraciously—science fiction, fantasy, romance, FBI thrillers and paranormal romances. She loves to spin wool into yarn, knit, crochet and learn new things.

Brian Busch is a freelance technical, marketing and fiction writer. Growing up in Wisconsin, he visited a seminary prep high school as a kid, and it serves as the backdrop for this story. The story is not autobiographical, however, and any names used in the story are purely fictional. Brian and his wife Jill have a daughter Natalie, and a son Paul, and they reside in Carver County.

S. Collin Ellsworth is the author of the novel, *Answered*. She has contributed to *Edina Magazine* and is the host of the upcoming podcast, "Ten Thousand Lakes, Ten Million Books."

David Gollin was trained in science, receiving a Ph.D. in Molecular Biology and Biochemistry from the University of Georgia. A crisis in his life brought him to his knees and it was only then that he began a process of connecting his faith and beliefs to his heart. His writing has focused on his spiritual walk from self-centered obsession to God-centered peace. Visit hearttransformed.com.

Bethany Hammer is a lover of words and story, who sees books as inns with candles in the windows, waiting. One of her favorite literary lines is found in C.S. Lewis's book, *Till We Have Faces*. "The sweetest thing in all my life has been the longing... to find the place where all the beauty comes from..."

Susana Hansen's passion for classical music intertwines with her passion for writing as she enjoys examining the complexities of what happens "behind the curtain" in the lives of composers and classical singers. Susana discovered her love of poetry while taking creative writing coursework at Wichita State University. She has studied under Albert Goldbarth, Sam Taylor, and Ed Skoog.

Angela Hunt started writing after a brain injury limited verbal communication. A librarian and speaker, she promotes writing and public presentation to help others. Her four books: *My Father in Verse, Am I Still Me?*; *Way Out on a Limb*; *I Am Still Me!*; *now Concerning War: A Collection of Recollections with Room for Rumination* is in the throes of formatting.

Anne Jackson: I am the mother of two delightful hooligans, married to a great guy and I work full time. When I figure out how to balance everything I will tell you how, for a price. My manifesto would be something about never letting the person you always thought you would be die...if I had time to write it.

James Robert Kane is enjoying retirement writing stories about love lost and rediscovered, murder, blackmail, sex, death and the struggle for reconciliation with God, often inspired by downright spooky phenomenon. He has four self-published e-books on Amazon and traditionally published short stories, *Screams* and *Sex and Sister Margaret*. He and his very understanding wife live in Chaska.

Sue Kunitz: I have been writing since 6th grade. I write songs, sing, act, perform, and have acted in plays my Mother wrote. The most recent being Crocerdile Betty with my Mom's Crocedillon Thomas. Poems/journal writing come to me daily. They are handwritten, then typed.

Michael Lein grew up in small towns across south western Minnesota. Bemidji State University then lured him north for a degree and graduate work in Environmental studies. Mike is currently the Environmental Services Manager for Carver County in Chaska, MN. He is also a freelance writer with creative nonfiction articles published in many regional and national magazines.

Chris Lemke is a committed founding member of the Chanhassen Writer's Group but, as these things tend to work themselves out, is only a casual writer. A native of Chanhassen, he invests his worldly interests in many different places. He currently studies at the University of Minnesota.

Becky Liestman is a former resident of the Writer's Room in NYC. Her poem "Father" was a winner in the Austin Texas International Poetry Festival. She has been published in its anthology many times. She was also a winner in The Crossings Poet Artist Collaboration. She is widely published in poetry journals and anthologies.

Diane Popovich Lynch is an environmental manager with over 25 years of experience managing projects in natural and water resources. She has published numerous creative non-fiction as well as business-related articles in a variety of publications. Her first book, *Minnesota Winery Stories*, was inspired by living in Oregon's wine country and was published by North Star Press in 2014.

Wen Lu came from China in 1986. She earned a Ph.D. degree in Chemistry and has worked as a scientist in the medical device industry. She has published numerous scientific journal articles and holds multiple patents in chemistry, biochemistry, and medicine.

D. E. Munson is also author of *By the Time I Got There*, a novel detailing the antics of Space Larrabee in his quest for meaning in life. Munson is also an award-winning poet, copywriter, graphic designer, guest speaker, folksinger, and has a blog at lunchonthemoon.com.

Dan O'Brien [MA in Advanced Japanese Studies] is author of the Japan Series, "Exploring Japanese culture through mysteries." (www.japanseries.com) He founded the Authors Collective, a group of authors that collaborates to mutually enhance and nurture writing that is stimulating, creative, and informative. A member of the Chahassen Library Writer's Group since 2011, he coordinates and participates in public readings for writers. He has read at coffee shops, literary art centers, and bookstores around Minnesota.

Carol Scott: The poetry of Carol Scott is an eclectic mix of subjects but full of unmistakable visual imagery and sound bites that delight the imagination as well as the ears. Having been involved in writing poetry for over 20 years, she is quick to recognize how her poems are evolving. Carol and husband, Tom, are recent transplants from Eastern Kentucky.

Virginia Sievers: "Waiting" is the first story in *Waiting: a Collective*. It won First Prize for Short Story in the 2013 Arizona Literary Contest. The book is available on Amazon. com as is the author's new book, *No Dancing in the Kitchen: a Collective*.

Heidi Skarie writes visionary novels filled with action, adventure and romance, featuring strong heroes and heroines. *Star Rider on the Razor's Edge* is her first science fiction novel. "Interrupted Honeymoon" takes place between the first and second novel in the series. She also writes historical novels including *Red Willow's Quest* and *Annoure and the Dragon Ships*.

B.D. Smith: a poet living in Chaska, and lifelong resident of Minnesota. My writing focuses on giving the reader snap shots of the world I live in. My intent to share thoughts and ideas that you may find interesting and enlightening, experiences that may open your mind to another personís point of view. I hope that you enjoy the work I have added to the anthology.

Dale Swanson is a published author, playwright and poet. His historical novel, *The Thirty-ninth Man* was listed in the *Star Tribune* reader survey for best book in 2013. Two of his radio plays have aired statewide. His middle grade fantasy chapter book, *Wild Ways—Mystery of the Hanging Tower*, was released in December 2015 and is moving up the charts.

Made in the USA
Lexington, KY
29 April 2017